Common Core Lessons

Reading
Literary Text

Grade **3**

Editorial Development: Barbara Allman
Lisa Vitarisi Mathews
Copy Editing: Cathy Harber
Art Direction: Cheryl Puckett
Art Manager: Kathy Kopp
Cover Design: Yuki Meyer
Illustration: Doris Ettlinger
Ann Iosa
Gary Mohrman
Design/Production: Carolina Caird
Jessica Onken

EMC 3213

Evan-Moor®

Helping Children Learn

Visit
teaching-standards.com
to view a correlation
of this book.
This is a free service.

**Correlated to State and
Common Core State Standards**

**Congratulations on your purchase of some of the
finest teaching materials in the world.**

For information about other Evan-Moor products, call 1-800-777-4362,
fax 1-800-777-4332, or visit our Web site, www.evan-moor.com.
Entire contents © 2015 EVAN-MOOR CORP.
18 Lower Ragsdale Drive, Monterey, CA 93940-5746. Printed in USA.

CPSIA: Printed by McNaughton & Gunn, Saline, MI USA. [1/2015]

Contents

Introduction

What's in Every Unit? 4

Correlations: *Common Core State Standards* 6

Correlations: *Texas Essential Knowledge and Skills* 8

Overview of Texts 11

Reproducible Reference Charts:

    Literary Genres 12

    Literary Elements and Story Structure 13

Units

Aesop's Fable

L Country Mouse and City Mouse 14

Mystery

M How Do You Spell *Beware*? 26

Folk Tale

M The Mitten

Adapted from *A Folk Tale from Ukraine* by E. Rachev 38

Classic Fiction

N Rebecca's School Day

Adapted from *Rebecca from Sunnybrook Farm* by Kate Douglas Wiggin 50

Fairy Tale

N Never Kick a Slipper at the Moon

Adapted from *Rootabaga Stories* by Carl Sandburg 62

Tall Tale

O Davy Crockett Escapes a Tornado

Adapted from Davy Crockett's *1846 Almanac* 74

Poetry and Song

O The New-England Boy's Song About Thanksgiving Day 86

Historical Fiction

P Lunch with Diego 98

Greek Legend

P Damon and Pythias 110

What's in Every Unit?

Teacher Resource Pages

The teacher's pages provide lesson preparation and instructional guidance.

The unit overview includes:

- The guided reading level
- Lesson objectives
- A suggested learning path
- Common Core State Standards citations

The teaching path includes:

- Suggested pacing
- Instructional guidance for having students complete the activities

The Close Reading Discussion includes:

- Scripted questions and sample responses about the literary selection

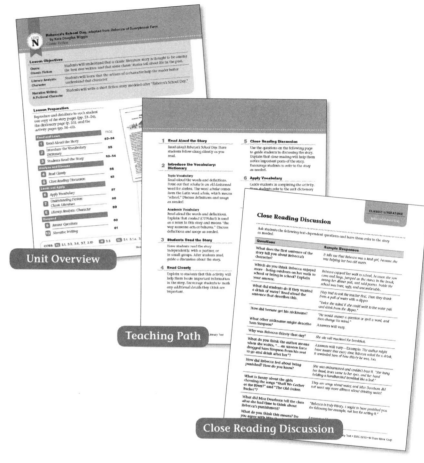

Unit Overview

Teaching Path

Close Reading Discussion

Literary Selections

The stories and poems include a variety of fiction genres and provide a range of literary experiences.

Fiction genres include:

- Aesop's Fable
- Mystery
- Folk Tale
- Classic Fiction
- Fairy Tale
- Tall Tale
- Historical Fiction
- Greek Legend

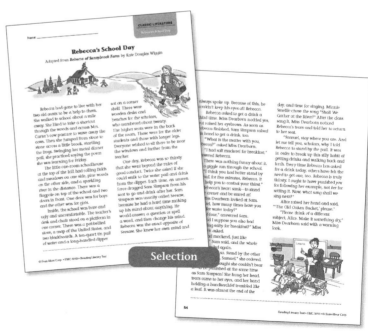

Selection

Student Pages

The activity pages help students understand vocabulary, focus on genre characteristics and literary elements, and write about the selection.

Dictionary—Defines topic and academic vocabulary words to help students better understand their use in the story or poem.

Read Closely—Guides students to interact with the text and identify important information.

Apply Vocabulary—Provides students another opportunity to interact with key words from the story or poem and apply them in a different context.

Understanding Fiction: Genre—Guides students to examine the genre's characteristics and techniques within the selection.

Literary Analysis—Guides students to examine literary elements within the selection.

Answer Questions—Asks students to answer questions about key ideas and details in the selection.

Literary Response/Narrative Writing—Provides students with a focused writing prompt about the selection.

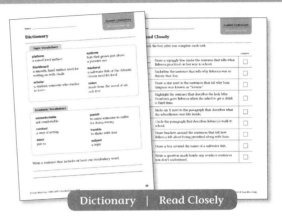

Dictionary | Read Closely

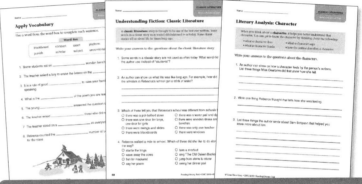

Apply Vocabulary | Understanding Fiction | Literary Analysis

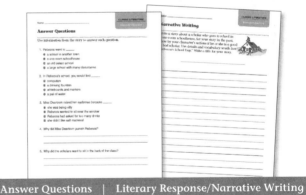

Answer Questions | Literary Response/Narrative Writing

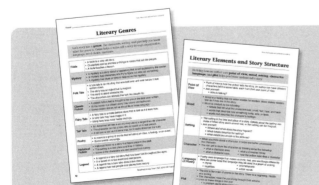

Student Reference Charts

Literary Genres
A reproducible chart lists fiction genres and explains the characteristics of each genre.

Literary Elements and Story Structure
A reproducible chart describes how authors use literary elements and story structure.

Correlations: Common Core State Standards

Units

Reading Standards for Literature, Grade 3	Country Mouse and City Mouse	How Do You Spell *Beware?*	The Mitten	Rebecca's School Day	Never Kick a Slipper at the Moon	Davy Crockett Escapes a Tornado	The New-England Boy's Song About Thanksgiving Day	Lunch with Diego	Damon and Pythias
Key Ideas and Details									
3.1 Ask and answer questions to demonstrate understanding of a text, referring explicitly to the text as the basis for the answers.	•	•	•	•	•	•	•	•	•
3.2 Recount stories, including fables, folk tales, and myths from diverse cultures; determine the central message, lesson, or moral and explain how it is conveyed through key details in the text.	•		•			•			•
3.3 Describe characters in a story (e.g., their traits, motivations, or feelings) and explain how their actions contribute to the sequence of events.	•	•	•	•		•			•
Craft and Structure									
3.4 Determine the meaning of words and phrases as they are used in a text, distinguishing literal from nonliteral language.		•				•			•
3.5 Refer to parts of stories, dramas, and poems when writing or speaking about a text, using terms such as *chapter*, *scene*, and *stanza*; describe how each successive part builds on earlier sections.		•							
3.6 Distinguish their own point of view from that of the narrator or those of the characters.	•			•		•	•		•
Integration of Knowledge and Ideas									
3.7 Explain how specific aspects of a text's illustrations contribute to what is conveyed by the words in a story (e.g., create mood, emphasize aspects of a character or setting).	•	•	•	•	•	•	•	•	•
Range of Reading and Level of Text Complexity									
3.10 By the end of the year, read and comprehend literature, including stories, dramas, and poetry, at the high end of the grades 2–3 text complexity band independently and proficiently.	•	•	•	•	•	•	•	•	•

Reading Literary Text • EMC 3213 • © Evan-Moor Corp.

Correlations: Common Core State Standards

Units

Writing Standards for Grade 3	Country Mouse and City Mouse	How Do You Spell *Beware?*	The Mitten	Rebecca's School Day	Never Kick a Slipper at the Moon	Davy Crockett Escapes a Tornado	The New-England Boy's Song About Thanksgiving Day	Lunch with Diego	Damon and Pythias
Text Types and Purposes									
3.1 Write opinion pieces on topics or texts, supporting a point of view with reasons.			●			●			●
3.2 Write informative/explanatory texts to examine a topic and convey ideas and information clearly.		●						●	
3.3 Write narratives to develop real or imagined experiences or events using effective techniques, descriptive details, and clear event sequences.*	●			●	●		●*narrative poetry		

Speaking and Listening Standards for Grade 3	Country Mouse and City Mouse	How Do You Spell *Beware?*	The Mitten	Rebecca's School Day	Never Kick a Slipper at the Moon	Davy Crockett Escapes a Tornado	The New-England Boy's Song About Thanksgiving Day	Lunch with Diego	Damon and Pythias
Comprehension and Collaboration									
3.1 Engage effectively in a range of collaborative discussions (one-on-one, in groups, and teacher-led) with diverse partners on grade 3 topics and texts, building on others' ideas and expressing their own clearly.	●	●	●	●	●	●	●	●	●
3.1a Come to discussions prepared, having read or studied required material; explicitly draw on that preparation and other information known about the topic to explore ideas under discussion.	●	●	●	●	●	●	●	●	●
3.2 Determine the main ideas and supporting details of a text read aloud or information presented in diverse media and formats, including visually, quantitatively, and orally.	●	●	●	●	●	●	●	●	●

Correlations:
Texas Essential Knowledge and Skills

Units

Texas Essential Knowledge and Skills	Country Mouse and City Mouse	How Do You Spell Beware?	The Mitten	Rebecca's School Day	Never Kick a Slipper at the Moon	Davy Crockett Escapes a Tornado	The New-England Boy's Song About Thanksgiving Day	Lunch with Diego	Damon and Pythias
110.14(b)(5) Reading/Comprehension of Literary Text/Theme and Genre. Students analyze, make inferences, and draw conclusions about theme and genre in different cultural, historical, and contemporary contexts and provide evidence from the text to support their understanding. Students are expected to:	•	•	•	•	•	•	•	•	•
(A) paraphrase the themes and supporting details of fables, legends, myths, or stories.	•								•
(110.14(b)(6) Reading/Comprehension of Literary Text/Poetry. Students understand, make inferences, and draw conclusions about the structure and elements of poetry and provide evidence from text to support their understanding. Students are expected to describe the characteristics of various forms of poetry and how they create imagery (e.g., narrative poetry, lyrical poetry, humorous poetry, free verse).							•		
110.14(b)(8) Reading/Comprehension of Literary Text/Fiction. Students understand, make inferences, and draw conclusions about the structure and elements of fiction and provide evidence from text to support their understanding. Students are expected to:	•	•	•	•	•	•	•	•	•
(A) sequence and summarize the plot's main events and explain their influence on future events;	•	•			•			•	•
(B) describe the interaction of characters including their relationships and the changes they undergo; and	•		•			•			•
(C) identify whether the narrator or speaker of a story is first or third person.	•	•				•	•	•	

Reading Literary Text • EMC 3213 • © Evan-Moor Corp.

Units

	Country Mouse and City Mouse	How Do You Spell Beware?	The Mitten	Rebecca's School Day	Never Kick a Slipper at the Moon	Davy Crockett Escapes a Tornado	The New-England Boy's Song About Thanksgiving Day	Lunch with Diego	Damon and Pythias
110.14(b)(10) **Reading/Comprehension of Literary Text/Sensory Language.** Students understand, make inferences, and draw conclusions about how an author's sensory language creates imagery in literary text and provide evidence from text to support their understanding. Students are expected to identify language that creates a graphic visual experience and appeals to the senses.	•	•			•	•	•	•	
110.14(b)(18) **Writing/Literary Texts.** Students write literary texts to express their ideas and feelings about real or imagined people, events, and ideas. Students are expected to:	•		•	•	•	•		•	•
(A) write imaginative stories that build the plot to a climax and contain details about the characters and setting; and	•			•	•				
(B) write poems that convey sensory details using the conventions of poetry (e.g., rhyme, meter, patterns of verse).							•		
110.14(29) **Listening and Speaking/Listening.** Students use comprehension skills to listen attentively to others in formal and informal settings. Students continue to apply earlier standards with greater complexity.	•	•	•	•	•	•	•	•	•

Overview of Texts

Title	Level	Genre	Literary Analysis	Writing Prompt
Country Mouse and City Mouse	L	Aesop's Fable	Point of View	Narrative
How Do You Spell *Beware*?	M	Mystery	Mood	Informative/ Explanatory
The Mitten	M	Folk Tale	Setting	Opinion
Rebecca's School Day	N	Classic Fiction	Character	Narrative
Never Kick a Slipper at the Moon	N	Fairy Tale	Setting	Narrative
Davy Crockett Escapes a Tornado	O	Tall Tale	Character	Opinion
The New-England Boy's Song About Thanksgiving Day	O	Poetry and Song	Language of Poetry	Narrative
Lunch with Diego	P	Historical Fiction	Plot	Informative/ Explanatory
Damon and Pythias	P	Greek Legend	Plot	Opinion

Name: _____

Literary Genres

Each story has a **genre**. The characters, setting, and plot help you know what the genre is. Genre helps a writer tell a story through organization, language, word choice, and voice.

Fable	• A fable is a very old story. • Characters can be animals or things in nature that act like people. • A fable teaches a lesson.
Mystery	• A mystery is a story about a happening that is not explained to the reader. • A mystery has characters who try to figure out who did something. • A mystery has clues or hints to help solve the mystery.
Folk Tale	• A folk tale is an old story that was told over and over before it was written down. • The story has an object that is magical. • The story is about everyday life. • The characters are animals that talk like people do.
Classic Fiction	• A classic fiction text is thought to be one of the best ever written. • Some words in a classic story may sound old-fashioned. • Some classic stories tell us about life in times long ago.
Fairy Tale	• A fairy tale is a make-believe story that is told as if it were true. • A fairy tale may have magic in it. • Many fairy tales have happy endings.
Tall Tale	• An American tall tale is an old story about a larger-than-life character. • The character can be a hero who is based on a real person. • A tall tale is told as if it were true, but it really stretches the truth.
Poetry	• A poem is a group of words that tell about an idea, a feeling, or an event. • Some poems are songs.
Historical Fiction	• Historical fiction is a story that takes place in the past. • The setting is a real place and time in history. • Some of the characters are real people from history.
Legend	• A legend is a very old story that has been told throughout the ages. • It is based on a real event and real people. • A legend has a hero who does brave deeds. • A legend has real people and places from history.

Name: _____

Literary Elements and Story Structure

Noticing how an author uses **point of view**, **mood**, **setting**, **character**, **language**, and **plot** helps you better understand a story.

Point of View	• Point of view is how the author tells the story. An author can have different characters tell the same fable, each from their own point of view. • Ask yourself: • Who is talking?

Mood	• Mood is a feeling that the writer creates for readers. Mood makes readers feel as if they are in the story.
	• Mood is created by the following:
	    • details that tell what the characters see, smell, feel, hear, and taste
	    • words that describe how something looks, acts, or feels
	    • words that describe the character's feelings

Setting	• The setting is the time and place of a story. Details about the setting can make a fiction story seem almost real, or the setting can be magical.
	• Ask yourself:
	    • Where and when does the story happen?
	    • What details describe the setting?
	    • What details are shown in the pictures?

Character	• When you think about a character, it helps you better understand the character.
	• You can get to know the character by thinking about the following:
	    • what a character does • what a character thinks
	    • what a character says • how the author describes a character

Language of Poetry	• Poetry uses language that makes us think, feel, and see things differently. Here are some ways that language may be used in a poem or a song:
	    • rhyme • onomatopoeia
	    • repetition • action words

Plot	• The plot is the order of events in the story. There is a beginning, middle, and ending.
	• The characters move the plot along through their actions.
	• Look for these things in the plot:
	    • A problem starts at the beginning.
	    • Something new happens in the middle.
	    • The problem is settled at the end of the story.

Country Mouse and City Mouse
Aesop's Fable

Lesson Objectives

Genre: Fable	Students will understand that a fable is a fiction story with animal characters that talk and act like people do and that it has a lesson at the end.
Literary Analysis: Point of View	Students will analyze different versions of the same fable to compare the points of view of different characters.
Narrative Writing: Story Writing	Students will write a short narrative about an imaginary experience, using a clear sequence of events and descriptive details.

Lesson Preparation

Reproduce and distribute to each student one copy of the story pages (pp. 17–18), the dictionary page (p. 19), and the activity pages (pp. 20–25).

Read and Learn   PAGE

1 Read Aloud the Fable   17–18

2 Introduce the Vocabulary
Dictionary   19

3 Students Read the Fable   17–18

Analyze and Discuss

4 *Read Closely*   20

5 *Close Reading Discussion*   16

Learn and Apply

6 *Apply Vocabulary*   21

7 *Understanding Fiction: Fable*   22

8 *Literary Analysis: Point of View*   23

Respond

9 *Answer Questions*   24

10 *Narrative Writing*
City Mouse's Visit   25

CCSS: **RL** 3.1, 3.2, 3.3, 3.6, 3.7, 3.10   **W** 3.3   **SL** 3.1, 3.1.a, 3.2

14   Reading Literary Text • EMC 3213 • © Evan-Moor Corp.

1 Read Aloud the Fable

Read aloud both versions of *Country Mouse and City Mouse.* Have students follow along silently as you read.

2 Introduce the Vocabulary: Dictionary

Topic Vocabulary
Read aloud the words and definitions. Point out that *hiss* is an example of onomatopoeia. Explain that this type of word sounds like the sound it is describing, as in the *hiss* of an angry cat. Discuss definitions and usage as needed.

Academic Vocabulary
Read aloud the words and definitions. Explain that *fancy* and *simple* have opposite meanings. This makes them antonyms. Then point out that *cozy* and *comfortable* mean about the same thing, so they are synonyms. Discuss definitions and usage as needed.

3 Students Read the Fable

Have students read both versions of the fable independently, with a partner, or in small groups. After students read, guide a discussion about the stories.

4 Read Closely

Explain to students that this activity will help them locate important information in the stories. Encourage students to mark any additional details they think are important.

5 Close Reading Discussion

Use the questions on the following page to guide students in discussing the stories. Explain that close reading will help them notice important parts of the stories. Encourage students to refer to the stories as needed.

6 Apply Vocabulary

Guide students in completing the activity. Have students refer to the unit dictionary as needed.

7 Understanding Fiction: Fable

Read aloud the description of a fable. Then guide students in completing the activity. Encourage them to refer to the stories as needed.

8 Literary Analysis: Point of View

Read aloud the description of how point of view affects a story. Then guide students in completing the activity, encouraging them to refer to the stories as needed.

9 Answer Questions

To ensure reading comprehension, have students answer the text-dependent questions. Review the answers together.

You may wish to use this activity as a formative assessment to determine students' understanding of the text.

10 Narrative Writing: *City Mouse's Visit*

Have students complete the writing activity independently, with a partner, or in small groups.

Close Reading Discussion

Ask students the following text-dependent questions and have them refer to the two versions of the fable as needed.

Compare Story 1 and Story 2. In what way are they the same?	*Both stories tell the same fable about Country Mouse and City Mouse.*
What is the main difference in how the two stories are told?	*Story 1 is told from the point of view of Country Mouse, and Story 2 is told from the point of view of City Mouse.*
Country Mouse was almost ready to consider moving to the city, until something happened. What was it?	*As the mice were having a feast, the cat entered the dining room and chased them. The mice had to run for their lives.*
What was different about the food that Country Mouse served from the food that City Mouse served?	Answers will vary—Example: *Country Mouse's food was simple and homegrown; City Mouse's food was from grocery stores and bakeries.*
Do you think Country Mouse would ever go back to the city again? Explain your answer.	Answers will vary—Example: *Country Mouse would probably never go back to the city because he fears for his life. He believes the cat would catch him. He wants to eat in peace.*
From City Mouse's point of view, why did his cousin return home to the country? Read aloud the sentence.	*"I guess he wasn't used to cats."*
City Mouse said, "Nuts and seeds are not my idea of a meal. I was already longing for home." What do you think the word "longing" means?	Answers will vary—Example: *The word **longing** probably means "wanting."*
What is the lesson of this fable?	*"It is better to eat a simple meal in peace than it is to eat a fancy meal in fear."*
Explain the lesson in your own words.	Answers will vary.
What could City Mouse have done differently in Story 2 to change the way the story ended?	Answers will vary—Example: *He could have removed the food from the table and taken it to a place where the cat could not reach them.*
What does the illustration in Story 2 tell you about City Mouse's house?	Answers will vary—Example: *City Mouse lives in a house with people who had a big dinner.*

Reading Literary Text • EMC 3213 • © Evan-Moor Corp.

Name: _____

Country Mouse and City Mouse
Story 1

I love my simple home in the country. I don't live like a king, but I'm comfortable and I don't go hungry. I like to scamper in the fields and among the trees with my friends.

One day my cousin, City Mouse, came to visit. It was a thrill to have a guest. I prepared a tasty supper of the best food I had stored away. There were dried seeds, beans, nuts, and fruits. There were even some old bacon bits and breadcrumbs. It was a feast fit for a Mouse King, if I do say so myself.

My cousin arrived on the big day and we greeted each other warmly. "Dear Cousin, I am so glad to see you," I said. "Please come and sit down, supper is ready."

No sooner did we sit down to supper than my cousin City Mouse turned up his nose. "Cousin dear, how can you eat this food? Come home with me and I'll show you how much better it is to live in the city."

He didn't have to ask twice. I had always wanted to visit the city. So off we went. It was quite late when we arrived. I followed my cousin inside. The house looked like a palace to me. The dining table was spread with what remained of a fancy dinner.

"Help yourself," my cousin said. I began to eat. The feast was far better than anything I had ever tasted. There were meats and cheeses, as well as cakes and jellies. I was thinking about moving to the city where I could enjoy this every day.

Suddenly, there was a loud scratching noise and the door flew open. Meow! Hiss! It was a very large, scary-looking cat. We had to run for our lives! I decided right then to go back to my cozy nest. *It is better to eat a simple meal in peace than it is to eat a fancy meal in fear.*

Name: _____

Country Mouse and City Mouse
Story 2

I grew up in the city and I live in a big house there. Things are always happening in the city. I love the way things move fast. There are new places to see and the finest foods to eat.

But one summer day, I decided it would be nice to take a trip. The country would be a nice change, quiet and restful, I thought. I could visit my cousin, Country Mouse!

When the day came for my trip, I hopped on a train and rode it out to the country. It was nice to see my dear cousin again. He's a simple mouse, but I love him just the same.

We sat down to have supper. The food was so plain and chewy that I could hardly eat it! Nuts and seeds are not my idea of a meal. I was already longing for home. So, I said, "Cousin, why don't you come home with me? I could show you how much better it is to live in the city."

It wasn't hard to talk my cousin into going with me to the city. We arrived home late, so I took him right into the dining room for something to eat. Because it was Friday night, I knew the table would have plenty of fine food left over from a big dinner.

We feasted on meats and cheeses, fine cakes, and jellies. Until the cat arrived, that is! That old cat was as mean as ever. He gave a hiss and a howl and began to chase us. My poor cousin and I ran for our lives! Country Mouse went back to the country that very same night. I guess he wasn't used to cats. He said *he would rather eat a simple meal in peace than eat a fancy meal in fear.*

Name: _____

Dictionary

Topic Vocabulary

scamper
to run or move quickly

cousin
a child of one's aunt or uncle

guest
a person who visits someone's home

breadcrumbs
tiny pieces of bread

hiss
to make a sound like the sound of the letter *s*

Academic Vocabulary

simple
plain; not fancy

comfortable
giving comfort or ease

thrill
a feeling of joy or excitement

fancy
not plain or simple

cozy
warm and snug

Write a sentence that includes at least one vocabulary word.

_____

_____

Name: _____

Read Closely

Check the box after you complete each task.

		Complete
~	Draw a squiggly line under the sentences in Story 1 that tell what Country Mouse prepared for supper.	☐
—	Underline the sentence in Story 2 that tells what City Mouse thinks about his cousin.	☐
★	Draw a star next to the sentence in Story 1 that tells what City Mouse did when he tasted the supper.	☐
🖍	Highlight any sentences in Story 1 and Story 2 that describe the cat.	☐
▲	Draw a triangle next to the sentence in Story 1 that tells what Country Mouse was beginning to consider before he saw the cat.	☐
✖	Make an X next to the sentence in Story 2 that explains why City Mouse knew there would be plenty to eat.	☐
○	In Story 1, circle the word that Country Mouse uses to describe the house in the city.	☐
[ ]	Draw brackets around the sentence in Story 1 and Story 2 that tells what the mice did when they saw the cat.	☐
?	Write a question mark beside any words or sentences you don't understand.	☐

Reading Literary Text • EMC 3213 • © Evan-Moor Corp.

Name: _____

Apply Vocabulary

Use a word from the word box to complete each sentence.

Word Box

comfortable	cousin	fancy	guest
hiss	scamper	simple	thrill

1. We saw a mouse _____ across the dining table.

2. He lives in a _____ little house in the country.

3. Will you be our _____ at supper tonight?

4. The cat made a loud _____ at the dog.

5. Their special cakes are very fine and _____.

6. His younger _____ lives in the country, too.

7. We ate a _____ meal of cheese and fruit.

8. It must be a _____ to visit the city.

Name: _____

Understanding Fiction: Fable

A **fable** is a fiction story with animal characters. Look for the following:

- animal characters that talk and act like people
- a lesson stated at the end of the story

Write your answers to the questions about the fable.

1. A different animal character tells each story. Reread the first paragraph of Story 1. Write the sentence that tells you Country Mouse is talking.

   _____

2. Reread the first paragraph of Story 2. Write the sentence that tells you City Mouse is talking.

   _____

   _____

3. Country Mouse prepared his best food. City Mouse did not have good manners. What words from the story show this?

   _____

   _____

4. What is the lesson stated at the end of the story?

   _____

   _____

5. Mark each detail that describes how the mice act like people.
   - ○ they talk
   - ○ they visit each other
   - ○ they have jobs
   - ○ they drive cars
   - ○ they wear clothes
   - ○ they have children

Name: _____

Literary Analysis: Point of View

Point of view is how an author tells a story. The same fable can be told from different points of view. Ask yourself: Who is talking?

- An author can have different characters tell the same fable, each from their own point of view.

Write your answers to the questions about the two ways of telling the fable.

1. From the point of view of Country Mouse, which foods make a feast fit for a Mouse King? List them.

   _____

   _____

2. What was City Mouse's point of view about his cousin's meal?

   _____

   _____

3. From the point of view of Country Mouse, what did the house in the city look like?

   _____

   _____

4. From the point of view of City Mouse, what caused his cousin to return home?

   _____

   _____

Name: _____

Answer Questions

Use information from the fable to answer each question.

1. City Mouse thought that _____.

    Ⓐ it is better to live in the city than in the country

    Ⓑ the country is a better place to live

    Ⓒ his cousin made a fancy supper

    Ⓓ things move too fast in the city

2. Story 1 and Story 2 _____.

    Ⓐ have different characters

    Ⓑ tell the same fable in different ways

    Ⓒ teach different lessons

    Ⓓ have different authors

3. Country Mouse thought that _____.

    Ⓐ his home in the country was too simple

    Ⓑ he should move to the city after all

    Ⓒ he didn't want to work at preparing food

    Ⓓ it was a thrill to have a supper guest

4. What did City Mouse think about his cousin?

    _____

    _____

5. Why did Country Mouse change his mind about living in the city once
   he got there?

    _____

    _____

Narrative Writing

··

What would happen if City Mouse went to visit another cousin in a faraway place? Would he like the food there? Choose one of the characters below or make up your own. Then write a story that tells what happens when City Mouse visits him.

- Desert Mouse   • Beach Mouse   • Zoo Mouse

City Mouse's Visit

_____

_____

_____

_____

_____

_____

_____

_____

_____

_____

_____

_____

_____

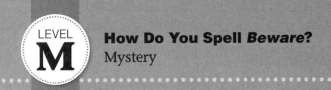

Lesson Objectives

Genre: Mystery	Students will understand that a mystery is about a happening that is not explained to the reader and that a character uses clues to solve the mystery.
Literary Analysis: Mood	Students will understand that the mood of a story is created by details and descriptions in the story.
Literary Response: Writing to Explain	Students will write an explanation of why the children were scared, giving supporting details from the story.

Lesson Preparation

Reproduce and distribute to each student one copy of the story pages (pp. 29–30), the dictionary page (p. 31), and the activity pages (pp. 32–37).

Read and Learn	PAGE
1 Read Aloud the Story	**29–30**
2 Introduce the Vocabulary *Dictionary*	**31**
3 Students Read the Story	**29–30**
Analyze and Discuss	
4 *Read Closely*	**32**
5 *Close Reading Discussion*	**28**
Learn and Apply	
6 *Apply Vocabulary*	**33**
7 *Understanding Fiction: Mystery*	**34**
8 *Literary Analysis: Mood*	**35**
Respond	
9 Answer Questions	**36**
10 *Literary Response* The Creepy House	**37**

CCSS: **RL** 3.1, 3.3, 3.4, 3.5, 3.7, 3.10   **W** 3.2   **SL** 3.1, 3.1.a, 3.2

1 Read Aloud the Story

Read aloud *How Do You Spell* Beware? Have students follow along silently as you read.

2 Introduce the Vocabulary: Dictionary

Topic Vocabulary
Read aloud the words and definitions. Point out that *cereal* begins with a soft *c* sound, /s/. Then explain that the word *beware* is what people say or use to warn others about something dangerous or scary, as in a "Beware of the Dog" sign. Discuss definitions and usage as needed.

Academic Vocabulary
Read aloud the words and definitions. Explain that *stale* can also describe how something tastes. Point out that *peer* has different meanings. In this story, it means "to take a close look at something." Discuss definitions and usage as needed.

3 Students Read the Story

Have students read the story independently, with a partner, or in small groups. After students read, guide a discussion about the story.

4 Read Closely

Explain to students that this activity will help them locate important information in the story. Encourage students to mark any additional details they think are important.

5 Close Reading Discussion

Use the questions on the following page to guide students in discussing the story. Explain that close reading will help them notice important parts of the story. Encourage students to refer to the story as needed.

6 Apply Vocabulary

Guide students in completing the activity. Have students refer to the unit dictionary as needed.

7 Understanding Fiction: Mystery

Read aloud the description of a mystery story. Then guide students in completing the activity. Encourage them to refer to the story as needed.

8 Literary Analysis: Mood

Read aloud the description of how an author creates mood. Then guide students in completing the activity, encouraging them to refer to the story as needed.

9 Answer Questions

To ensure reading comprehension, have students answer the text-dependent questions. Review the answers together.

You may wish to use this activity as a formative assessment to determine students' understanding of the text.

10 Literary Response: *The Creepy House*

Have students complete the writing activity independently, with a partner, or in small groups.

Close Reading Discussion

Ask students the following text-dependent questions and have them refer to the story as needed.

Questions	Sample Responses
How would you describe the house from looking at the picture?	Examples: *old, creepy, big*
What happened to the house when autumn came?	*The house grew dark after school and the windows rattled on windy nights.*
What did Bradley tell his sisters in order to try to scare them?	*He told them there were lots of places for ghosts to hide in the house. He told them to tap on the wall or scream if they saw a ghost.*
What is the mood of the story?	Examples: *spooky, scary, mysterious*
What words in the story create the mood?	"empty," "stale," "dust," "icky," "cobwebs," "ghosts," "scare," "hide," "scream," "creepy," "cold and windy"
Why does Clare think that Bradley is trying to scare her with the note?	*Because Bradley has tried to scare her and their sister before.*
Why might Bradley think that Clare is trying to scare him with the word "beware" on the kitchen table?	*She may be trying to get him back for scaring her earlier.*
Why does Clare tell Bradley to keep the note a secret from Lily?	*Clare thinks Lily will be scared if she sees the note.*
What clue solved the mystery? How?	*The backward letter **a** in **beware** solved the mystery, because Lily writes it that way. The children's mom pointed it out.*
What were the main events in the plot?	*The family moved into the old house, Bradley teased the girls about ghosts, and Clare and Bradley started finding the word **beware** written around the house and a note.*
Did the main events give you clues about how the story might end?	Answers will vary.
Is this story told in the first person or the third person? Give an example.	*This story is told in the third person.* Answers will vary—Example: *"Bradley, Clare, and Lily were moving into a new home with their mom."*
The author wrote, "The house moaned..." Is this literal or nonliteral language? Explain your answer.	*This is nonliteral language, because a house cannot speak.*

How Do You Spell *Beware?*

It was summer break. Bradley, Clare, and Lily were moving into a new home with their mom. The house was over a hundred years old and had stood empty for years. There was a cemetery next to it.

As they entered the old house, they noticed a stale smell and saw lots of dust. Clare's nose tickled, which made her sneeze. "Don't you love this old house?" their mom asked.

"I like it," said Lily. "But I don't like all the icky cobwebs."

"This house is huge," said Bradley. "I guess it gives the ghosts more places to hide."

"You always try to scare me, Bradley!" said Clare.

"Who's ready for lunch?" asked Mom.

After lunch, the children chose their bedrooms and unpacked.

That night, Bradley told Clare and Lily, "I'm in the next room. Just tap on the wall if you see a ghost . . . or scream!"

"Bradley!" shouted Clare and Lily. They didn't like it when Bradley scared them, but they had to admit that the house was creepy.

Summer passed quickly and school started again. Autumn was cold and windy, and the windows of the old house rattled.

One night, as the children were doing homework, Lily asked Clare, "Can you help me with my spelling words? Some of them are hard."

"Okay," said Clare. "An easy way to learn how to spell is to write the hard words over and over."

"That's good advice, Clare," said Bradley. "Here's one for practice—g-h-o-s-t."

"Bradley!" yelled Clare.

The kids finished their homework and went to bed. It was a windy night. The house moaned and the windows rattled.

The next day when Bradley and Clare got home from school, the house was dark. They couldn't find their mom or Lily anywhere. Then Clare remembered that Mom had taken Lily to her dance lesson.

"Hey, what's this on the floor?" asked Bradley. "It looks like Mom left us a note."

"What does it say?" asked Clare.

"It says *beware*," replied Bradley. The word *beware* was written in shaky handwriting.

"Let me see that," said Clare. "You're just trying to scare me."

"I am not," said Bradley. "I've never seen this note before."

The kids were spooked. Who had written the message? Had the note been on top of the cupboard for years and just now fallen down?

"Don't tell Lily about the note," said Clare. "It will scare her."

Later, Clare and Bradley were in their rooms doing homework. Bradley felt hungry, so he went to the kitchen for a bowl of cereal. As he sat down to eat, he noticed a word on the table spelled with cereal—b-e-w-a-r-e.

He quickly called Clare into the kitchen and blamed her for trying to scare him. Clare said she had nothing to do with it.

The next night, Lily and Mom were in the kitchen while Bradley and Clare watched television. Suddenly, Clare screamed, "Bradley, look!" The word *beware* was written in the frost on the window. Bradley and Clare froze with fear. Now they were *sure* that a ghost was in their house.

They called out to their mom. "What's the matter?" she asked, running in.

The kids explained that they had seen the word *beware* written around the house during the past few days. Their mom peered at the window.

"Hmm…the letter *a* is backward," she said. "Who writes the letter *a* backward?"

"Lily!" shouted Clare and Bradley. At that moment, Lily walked into the room and said, "Clare told me to write the hard spelling words over and over again. I'm trying to learn how to spell the word *beware*."

Name: _____

Dictionary

Topic Vocabulary

cemetery
a place where the dead are
buried

cobweb
threads of a spider web covered
with dust

rattle
to make a series of short or
sharp sounds

beware
to be careful; to be on the watch
for something

cereal
a food made of grain, such as
cornflakes

Academic Vocabulary

stale
old, stuffy, or musty smelling

admit
to say or confess something
is true

advice
helpful ideas or tips

peer
to look closely at something

Write a sentence that includes at least one vocabulary word.

_____

_____

Read Closely

···

Check the box after you complete each task.

		Complete
~	Draw a squiggly line under the sentence that tells how old the house is.	☐
—	Underline the sentence that tells what the children smelled and saw when they entered the house.	☐
★	Draw a star next to the sentence that tells what is next to the house.	☐
✎	Highlight two words in the story that describe how the children felt.	☐
▲	Draw a triangle next to the sentence that tells what rattled the windows of the house.	☐
✖	Make an X next to the advice that Clare gave Lily about spelling.	☐
○	Circle the sentence that tells what the children heard one windy night.	☐
[ ]	Draw brackets around the sentence that tells why Clare screamed.	☐
?	Write a question mark beside any words or sentences you don't understand.	☐

Name: _____

Apply Vocabulary

Use a word from the word box to complete each sentence.

Word Box			
admit	advice	beware	cemetery
cereal	cobweb	peer	rattle

1. The old house is next to a _____.

2. You can _____ inside through a window.

3. We didn't see the giant _____ and walked right into it!

4. All we had to eat for breakfast was _____.

5. The storm caused the doors and windows to _____.

6. We had to _____ that the house was creepy.

7. Take her _____ and do not be scared.

8. The sign on the gate said "_____ of the Dog!"

Understanding Fiction: Mystery

A **mystery** is a story about a happening that is not explained to the reader.
The mystery is solved at the very end of the story by one of the characters.
A mystery has these things:

- characters who try to figure out who did something
- clues or hints to help solve the mystery

Write your answers to the questions about the mystery story.

1. What did Bradley find on the floor one day?

   _____

   _____

2. Clare thought that Bradley was trying to scare her with the note. How else
   did they try to explain the note?

   _____

   _____

3. What does Bradley think at first when he sees *beware* spelled with cereal?

   _____

   _____

4. What clue on the window points to Lily?

   _____

   _____

   _____

Literary Analysis: Mood

Mood is the feeling that a writer creates for readers. Mood makes readers feel as if they are there in the story. A mood is created by using:

- details that tell what characters see, smell, feel, hear, and taste
- words that describe how something looks, acts, or feels
- words that describe characters' feelings

Write your answers to the questions about the mood.

1. What words in the story describe the house?

   _____

   _____

2. What did the children see and smell in the house?

   _____

   _____

3. What could be heard in the old house?

   _____

   _____

4. What feelings did the children have throughout the story?

   _____

   _____

Name: _____

Answer Questions

Use information from the mystery story to answer each question.

1. Clare and Bradley tried to figure out _____.

    Ⓐ why the house had dust

    Ⓑ why the windows rattled

    Ⓒ how many ghosts there were

    Ⓓ who wrote the word *beware*

2. Clare and Bradley did not want to scare Lily, so they didn't show her the note. That is why _____.

    Ⓐ the house was huge

    Ⓑ the word was *beware*

    Ⓒ the mystery went on for days

    Ⓓ there was a cemetery

3. When autumn came, the house _____.

    Ⓐ became less scary

    Ⓑ was dark after school

    Ⓒ got warmer

    Ⓓ seemed bigger

4. The children were scared in the new house. Which character was <u>not</u> scared?

    _____

5. Explain why Clare and Bradley froze.

    _____

6. Why did Lily write *beware* so many times?

    _____

    _____

Name: _____

Literary Response

Explain why Clare and Bradley were scared in their new house. Use details from the story.

The Creepy House

_____

_____

_____

_____

_____

_____

_____

_____

_____

_____

_____

_____

_____

_____

_____

_____

LEVEL **M**

The Mitten, adapted from *A Folk Tale from Ukraine* by E. Rachev
Folk Tale

Lesson Objectives

Genre: Folk Tale   Students will understand that a folk tale is a story about everyday life and that it may have a magical object, a pattern, or animal characters that talk.

Literary Analysis: Setting   Students will identify the setting as the time and place of a story. Details in the text and pictures help describe the setting.

Literary Response: Opinion   Students will write an opinion that tells whether Mouse should or should not have let the other animals inside the mitten.

Lesson Preparation

Reproduce and distribute to each student one copy of the story pages (pp. 41–42), the dictionary page (p. 43), and the activity pages (pp. 44–49).

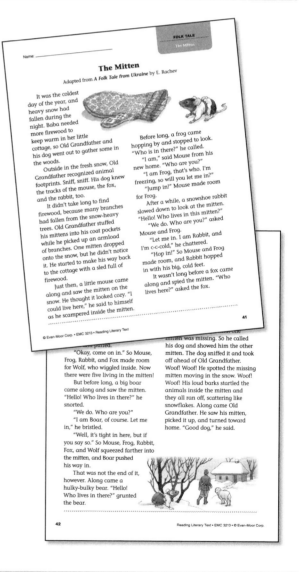

Read and Learn	PAGE
1 Read Aloud the Folk Tale	**41–42**
2 Introduce the Vocabulary *Dictionary*	**43**
3 Students Read the Folk Tale	**41–42**
Analyze and Discuss	
4 *Read Closely*	**44**
5 *Close Reading Discussion*	**40**
Learn and Apply	
6 *Apply Vocabulary*	**45**
7 *Understanding Fiction: Folk Tale*	**46**
8 *Literary Analysis: Setting*	**47**
Respond	
9 *Answer Questions*	**48**
10 *Literary Response*	**49**

CCSS: **RL** 3.1, 3.2, 3.3, 3.7, 3.10   **W** 3.1   **SL** 3.1, 3.1.a, 3.2

1 Read Aloud the Folk Tale

Read aloud *The Mitten.* Have students follow along silently as you read.

2 Introduce the Vocabulary: Dictionary

Topic Vocabulary

Read aloud the words and definitions. Point out that long ago, a *cottage* was the small house of a farmer or a peasant. Explain that the *snout* of an animal is its long nose, such as the snout of a pig. Ask students to name other animals with a snout. (e.g., dog, bear, fox) Discuss definitions and usage as needed.

Academic Vocabulary

Read aloud the words and definitions. Explain that *bristle* is both a noun and a verb. As a noun, it is a stiff hair, such as on a pig. Point out that in this story, it is used as a verb. If someone *bristles*, he stiffens like a bristle because he is upset. Discuss definitions and usage as needed.

3 Students Read the Folk Tale

Have students read the folk tale independently, with a partner, or in small groups. After students read, guide a discussion about the story.

4 Read Closely

Explain to students that this activity will help them locate important information in the story. Encourage students to mark any additional details they think are important.

5 Close Reading Discussion

Use the questions on the following page to guide students in discussing the folk tale. Explain that close reading will help them notice important parts of the story. Encourage students to refer to the story as needed.

6 Apply Vocabulary

Guide students in completing the activity. Have students refer to the unit dictionary as needed.

7 Understanding Fiction: Folk Tale

Read aloud the description of a folk tale. Then guide students in completing the activity. Encourage them to refer to the story as needed.

8 Literary Analysis: Setting

Read aloud the description of how the setting affects a story. Then guide students in completing the activity, encouraging them to refer to the story as needed.

9 Answer Questions

To ensure reading comprehension, have students answer the text-dependent questions. Review the answers together.

You may wish to use this activity as a formative assessment to determine students' understanding of the text.

10 Literary Response

Have students complete the writing activity independently, with a partner, or in small groups.

Close Reading Discussion

Ask students the following text-dependent questions and have them refer to the story as needed.

Questions	Sample Responses
Folk tales often have some magic in them. What things about this story are magical?	*The mitten grows big enough to hold seven animals. Also, the animals talk and act like people do.*
The smaller animals let the larger, scary animals into the mitten. What does this show about the animal characters?	*The animal characters are kind to each other. They move over to make room, maybe because they were cold once themselves.*
How do you know the story takes place in the winter? Support your answer by reading from the text.	*It is winter because the story takes place in a cold, snowy place on the coldest day of the year.* *"It was the coldest day of the year, and heavy snow had fallen during the night."*
Were Mouse's actions important in the story? Explain why or why not.	*Answers will vary—Example: Yes, Mouse's actions were important because he let the first animal into the mitten and that's how the story develops.*
Do you think that Old Grandfather knew about the animals in his mitten? Why or why not? Give evidence from the text.	*No, Old Grandfather didn't know, because the dog was ahead of him and scared away the animals before he came along.* *"His loud barks startled the animals inside the mitten and they all ran off, scattering like snowflakes. Along came Old Grandfather."* **OR** *Yes, he did know. Maybe he saw the animals scatter from a distance, and said "Good dog" because the dog chased the animals away.*
"Baba" is another name for "grandmother." Where is the character of Baba throughout the story?	*She is at home in the cottage.*
How do you know from the pictures of Mouse that the characters in this story act like people?	*Mouse is wearing clothes.*
What lesson could you learn from this folk tale?	*Answers will vary—Example: One lesson could be to help everyone in need that you can.*

Reading Literary Text • EMC 3213 • © Evan-Moor Corp.

Name: _____

The Mitten

Adapted from *A Folk Tale from Ukraine* by E. Rachev

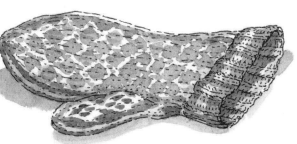

It was the coldest day of the year, and heavy snow had fallen during the night. Baba needed more firewood to keep warm in her little cottage, so Old Grandfather and his dog went out to gather some in the woods.

Outside in the fresh snow, Old Grandfather recognized animal footprints. Sniff, sniff. His dog knew the tracks of the mouse, the fox, and the rabbit, too.

It didn't take long to find firewood, because many branches had fallen from the snow-heavy trees. Old Grandfather stuffed his mittens into his coat pockets while he picked up an armload of branches. One mitten dropped onto the snow, but he didn't notice it. He started to make his way back to the cottage with a sled full of firewood.

Just then, a little mouse came along and saw the mitten on the snow. He thought it looked cozy. "I could live here," he said to himself as he scampered inside the mitten.

Before long, a frog came hopping by and stopped to look. "Who is in there?" he called.

"I am," said Mouse from his new home. "Who are you?"

"I am Frog, that's who. I'm freezing, so will you let me in?"

"Jump in!" Mouse made room for Frog.

After a while, a snowshoe rabbit slowed down to look at the mitten. "Hello! Who lives in this mitten?"

"We do. Who are you?" asked Mouse and Frog.

"Let me in. I am Rabbit, and I'm c-c-cold," he chattered.

"Hop in!" So Mouse and Frog made room, and Rabbit hopped in with his big, cold feet.

It wasn't long before a fox came along and spied the mitten. "Who lives here?" asked the fox.

"We do. Who are you?"

"I am Fox, and I have a cold snout. Will you let me in?"

"Certainly, make yourself at home." So Mouse, Frog, and Rabbit moved over and Fox slipped inside.

Next, a wolf happened along and saw the mitten. "Hello, my friends! Who lives in this mitten?" he asked.

"We do. Wh-wh-who are you?"

"I am Wolf. Let me in," he huffed and puffed.

"Okay, come on in." So Mouse, Frog, Rabbit, and Fox made room for Wolf, who wiggled inside. Now there were five living in the mitten!

But before long, a big boar came along and saw the mitten. "Hello! Who lives in there?" he snorted.

"We do. Who are you?"

"I am Boar, of course. Let me in," he bristled.

"Well, it's tight in here, but if you say so." So Mouse, Frog, Rabbit, Fox, and Wolf squeezed farther into the mitten, and Boar pushed his way in.

That was not the end of it, however. Along came a hulky-bulky bear. "Hello! Who lives in there?" grunted the bear.

"We do. Who are you?"

"I am Bear. Make room for me in there, would you?"

"Let us warn you, we are very crowded in here." But they all moved over and Bear squeezed inside. With seven, the mitten was about to burst!

Right about that time, Old Grandfather felt inside his coat pockets and realized that one mitten was missing. So he called his dog and showed him the other mitten. The dog sniffed it and took off ahead of Old Grandfather. Woof! Woof! He spotted the missing mitten moving in the snow. Woof! Woof! His loud barks startled the animals inside the mitten and they all ran off, scattering like snowflakes. Along came Old Grandfather. He saw his mitten, picked it up, and turned toward home. "Good dog," he said.

Name: _____

Dictionary

Topic Vocabulary

cottage
a small house in the country

snout
the long front part of an animal's head, including the nose, mouth, and jaws

boar
a wild pig

snort
to make a rough sound through the nose

hulky
large and clumsy

bulky
having great size or mass

Academic Vocabulary

recognize
to know and remember from before

scamper
to run quickly

bristle
to show signs of anger; to rise and stand up stiffly, like a bristle

startle
to cause to move suddenly with surprise or fright

scatter
to separate and go in different directions

Write a sentence that includes at least one vocabulary word.

_____

_____

Read Closely

Check the box after you complete each task.

		Complete
~	Draw a squiggly line under the sentence that tells why it was easy to find firewood.	☐
—	Underline the sentence that describes the day the story takes place.	☐
★	Draw a star next to the sentence that tells which animal found the mitten first.	☐
	The animals always ask the same question before letting a new animal into the mitten. Highlight the question each time it appears in the story.	☐
▲	Draw a triangle next to the sentence that describes how the animals in the mitten were startled.	☐
✖	Make an X next to the paragraph that explains how Old Grandfather told his dog to look for the mitten.	☐
○	Each animal in the story is bigger than the animal before it. Circle the name of the animal that is bigger than the boar.	☐
[ ]	Draw brackets around the sentences that tell what Old Grandfather did and said when he found his mitten.	☐
?	Write a question mark beside any words or sentences you don't understand.	☐

Name: _____

Apply Vocabulary

Use a word from the word box to complete each sentence.

Word Box

boar	bristle	bulky	cottage
recognize	scatter	snout	startle

1. Can you _____ the tracks of a wolf?

2. Baba and Old Grandfather live in a _____ near the woods.

3. The fox has a long _____ that turns up slightly.

4. The wind will _____ the leaves on the ground.

5. Did the dog _____ you when it barked?

6. The little girl wore a _____ coat to keep her warm.

7. They heard the _____ snorting loudly before they even saw it.

8. The man began to _____ when he saw that his car was missing.

Understanding Fiction: Folk Tale

A **folk tale** is an old story that was told over and over before it was written down. Look for these things in a folk tale:

- It has an object that is magical, such as a magic lamp.
- The story is about everyday life.
- It has a pattern.
- The characters are animals that talk like people do.

Write your answers to the questions about the folk tale.

1. What object in this story is magical?

   _____

2. In everyday life, people sometimes lose something, such as a mitten. What other thing did Old Grandfather do that was part of everyday life?

   _____

   _____

3. One by one, the animals went into the mitten to keep warm. If you drew the animals in story order, what pattern would you see?

   _____

   _____

4. List the animal characters that talk like people do. Which animal character does <u>not</u> talk?

   _____

   _____

Literary Analysis: Setting

The **setting** is the time and place of a story. Details about the setting can make a fiction story seem almost real, or the setting can be magical. Ask yourself:

- Where and when does the story happen?
- What details describe the setting?
- What details are shown in the pictures?

Write your answers to the questions about the setting.

1. The story begins inside a cottage in the woods. Where does the rest of the story take place?

   _____

   _____

2. The story takes place in wintertime. What two details about the time of year make the story seem real?

   _____

   _____

3. Ukraine is the country where this story was first told. What details do the pictures show about that place? Mark each answer.

   ○ clothes   ○ woods   ○ mountains

   ○ cities   ○ homes   ○ bears

4. What small object became a magical place? Why was it magical?

   _____

   _____

Answer Questions

Use information from the folk tale to answer each question.

1. Old Grandfather went out for firewood _____.
   Ⓐ but didn't find any
   Ⓑ but left his dog at home
   Ⓒ and dropped his mitten in the snow
   Ⓓ and became lost in the woods

2. Seven animals _____ to get warm.
   Ⓐ squeezed into the cottage
   Ⓑ crowded into the mitten
   Ⓒ found firewood
   Ⓓ went home

3. The animals _____.
   Ⓐ were kind to each other
   Ⓑ could not all fit in the mitten
   Ⓒ recognized footprints in the snow
   Ⓓ would not move over

4. What startled all the animals and made them run away?

   _____

   _____

5. What did the dog know that Old Grandfather may <u>not</u> have known?

   _____

   _____

Name: _____

Literary Response

Do you think that Mouse should have allowed the other animals to come inside the mitten? Write an opinion that tells why or why not. Use details from the story. Write a title.

_____

_____

_____

_____

_____

_____

_____

_____

_____

_____

_____

_____

_____

_____

LEVEL N

Rebecca's School Day, adapted from *Rebecca of Sunnybrook Farm*
by Kate Douglas Wiggin
Classic Fiction

Lesson Objectives

Genre: Classic Fiction	Students will understand that a classic literature story is thought to be among the best ever written and that some classic stories tell about life in the past.
Literary Analysis: Character	Students will learn that the actions of a character help the reader better understand that character.
Narrative Writing: A Fictional Character	Students will write a short fiction story modeled after "Rebecca's School Day."

Lesson Preparation

Reproduce and distribute to each student one copy of the story pages (pp. 53–54), the dictionary page (p. 55), and the activity pages (pp. 56–61).

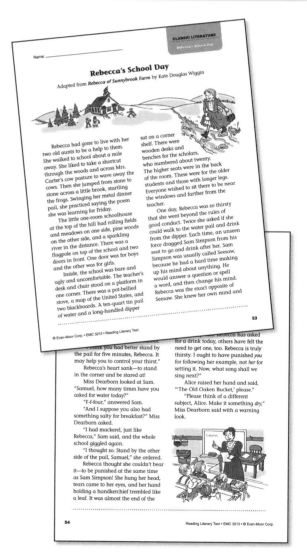

Read and Learn		PAGE
1	Read Aloud the Story	53–54
2	Introduce the Vocabulary *Dictionary*	55
3	Students Read the Story	53–54
Analyze and Discuss		
4	*Read Closely*	56
5	*Close Reading Discussion*	52
Learn and Apply		
6	*Apply Vocabulary*	57
7	*Understanding Fiction: Classic Literature*	58
8	*Literary Analysis: Character*	59
Respond		
9	*Answer Questions*	60
10	*Narrative Writing*	61

CCSS: **RL** 3.1, 3.3, 3.6, 3.7, 3.10   **W** 3.3   **SL** 3.1, 3.1.a, 3.2

1 Read Aloud the Story

Read aloud *Rebecca's School Day.* Have students follow along silently as you read.

2 Introduce the Vocabulary: Dictionary

Topic Vocabulary
Read aloud the words and definitions. Point out that *scholar* is an old-fashioned word for *student.* The word *scholar* comes from the Latin word *schola,* which means "school." Discuss definitions and usage as needed.

Academic Vocabulary
Read aloud the words and definitions. Explain that *conduct* (CONduct) is used as a noun in this story and means "the way someone acts or behaves." Discuss definitions and usage as needed.

3 Students Read the Story

Have students read the story independently, with a partner, or in small groups. After students read, guide a discussion about the story.

4 Read Closely

Explain to students that this activity will help them locate important information in the story. Encourage students to mark any additional details they think are important.

5 Close Reading Discussion

Use the questions on the following page to guide students in discussing the story. Explain that close reading will help them notice important parts of the story. Encourage students to refer to the story as needed.

6 Apply Vocabulary

Guide students in completing the activity. Have students refer to the unit dictionary as needed.

7 Understanding Fiction: Classic Literature

Read aloud the description of classic literature. Then guide students in completing the activity. Encourage them to refer to the story as needed.

8 Literary Analysis: Character

Read aloud the description of how to think about a character. Then guide students in completing the activity, encouraging them to refer to the story as needed.

9 Answer Questions

To ensure reading comprehension, have students answer the text-dependent questions. Review the answers together.

You may wish to use this activity as a formative assessment to determine students' understanding of the text.

10 Narrative Writing

Have students work independently, with a partner, or in small groups to write a short fiction story modeled after *Rebecca's School Day.*

Close Reading Discussion

Ask students the following text-dependent questions and have them refer to the story as needed.

Questions	Sample Responses
What does the first sentence of the story tell you about Rebecca's character?	*It tells me that Rebecca was a kind girl, because she was helping her two old aunts.*
Which do you think Rebecca enjoyed more—being outdoors on her walk to school or being in school? Explain your answer.	*Rebecca enjoyed her walk to school, because she saw cows and frogs, jumped on the stones in the brook, swung her dinner pail, and said poems. Inside the school was bare, ugly, and uncomfortable.*
What did students do if they wanted a drink of water? Read aloud the sentence that describes this.	*They had to ask the teacher first. Then they drank from a pail of water with a dipper.* *"Twice she asked if she could walk to the water pail and drink from the dipper."*
How did Seesaw get his nickname?	*"He would answer a question or spell a word, and then change his mind."*
What other nickname might describe Sam Simpson?	Answers will vary.
Why was Rebecca thirsty that day?	*She ate salt mackerel for breakfast.*
What do you think the author means when she writes, "…an unseen force dragged Sam Simpson from his seat to go and drink after her"?	Answers will vary—Example: *The author might have meant that every time Rebecca asked for a drink, it reminded Sam of how thirsty he was, too.*
How did Rebecca feel about being punished? How do you know?	*She was embarrassed and couldn't bear it. "She hung her head, tears came to her eyes, and her hand holding a handkerchief trembled like a leaf."*
What is funny about the girls choosing the songs "Shall We Gather at the River?" and "The Old Oaken Bucket"?	*They are songs about water, and Miss Dearborn did not want any more silliness about drinking water!*
What did Miss Dearborn tell the class after she had time to think about Rebecca's punishment?	*"Rebecca is truly thirsty. I ought to have punished you for following her example, not her for setting it."*
What do you think this means? Do you agree with Miss Dearborn?	Answers will vary.

Name: _____

Rebecca's School Day

Adapted from *Rebecca of Sunnybrook Farm* by Kate Douglas Wiggin

Rebecca had gone to live with her two old aunts to be a help to them. She walked to school about a mile away. She liked to take a shortcut through the woods and across Mrs. Carter's cow pasture to wave away the cows. Then she jumped from stone to stone across a little brook, startling the frogs. Swinging her metal dinner pail, she practiced saying the poem she was learning for Friday.

The little one-room schoolhouse at the top of the hill had rolling fields and meadows on one side, pine woods on the other side, and a sparkling river in the distance. There was a flagpole on top of the school and two doors in front. One door was for boys and the other was for girls.

Inside, the school was bare and ugly and uncomfortable. The teacher's desk and chair stood on a platform in one corner. There was a pot-bellied stove, a map of the United States, and two blackboards. A ten-quart tin pail of water and a long-handled dipper

sat on a corner shelf. There were wooden desks and benches for the scholars, who numbered about twenty. The higher seats were in the back of the room. These were for the older students and those with longer legs. Everyone wished to sit there to be near the windows and farther from the teacher.

One day, Rebecca was so thirsty that she went beyond the rules of good conduct. Twice she asked if she could walk to the water pail and drink from the dipper. Each time, an unseen force dragged Sam Simpson from his seat to go and drink after her. Sam Simpson was usually called Seesaw, because he had a hard time making up his mind about anything. He would answer a question or spell a word, and then change his mind. Rebecca was the exact opposite of Seesaw. She knew her own mind and always spoke up. Because of this, he couldn't keep his eyes off Rebecca.

Rebecca asked to get a drink a third time. Miss Dearborn nodded yes, but raised her eyebrows. As soon as Rebecca finished, Sam Simpson raised his hand to get a drink, too.

"What is the matter with you, Rebecca?" asked Miss Dearborn.

"I had salt mackerel for breakfast," answered Rebecca.

There was nothing funny about it, but a giggle ran through the school.

"I think you had better stand by the pail for five minutes, Rebecca. It may help you to control your thirst."

Rebecca's heart sank—to stand in the corner and be stared at!

Miss Dearborn looked at Sam. "Samuel, how many times have you asked for water today?"

"F-f-four," answered Sam.

"And I suppose you also had something salty for breakfast?" Miss Dearborn asked.

"I had mackerel, just like Rebecca," Sam said, and the whole school giggled again.

"I thought so. Stand by the other side of the pail, Samuel," she ordered.

Rebecca thought she couldn't bear it—to be punished at the same time as Sam Simpson! She hung her head, tears came to her eyes, and her hand holding a handkerchief trembled like a leaf. It was almost the end of the day, and time for singing. Minnie Smellie chose the song "Shall We Gather at the River?" After the class sang it, Miss Dearborn noticed Rebecca's tears and told her to return to her seat.

"Samuel, stay where you are. And let me tell you, scholars, why I told Rebecca to stand by the pail. It was in order to break up this silly habit of getting drinks and walking back and forth. Every time Rebecca has asked for a drink today, others have felt the need to get one, too. Rebecca is truly thirsty. I ought to have punished *you* for following her example, not *her* for setting it. Now, what song shall we sing next?"

Alice raised her hand and said, "'The Old Oaken Bucket,' please."

"Please think of a different subject, Alice. Make it something *dry*," Miss Dearborn said with a warning look.

Name: _____

Dictionary

Topic Vocabulary

platform
a raised level surface

blackboard
a smooth, hard surface used for writing on with chalk

scholar
a student; someone who studies to learn

eyebrow
hair that grows just above a person's eye

mackerel
a saltwater fish of the Atlantic Ocean used for food

oaken
made from the wood of an oak tree

Academic Vocabulary

uncomfortable
not comfortable

conduct
a way of acting

exact
just so

punish
to cause someone to suffer for doing wrong

tremble
to shake with fear

subject
a topic

Write a sentence that includes at least one vocabulary word.

_____

_____

Name: _____

Read Closely

Check the box after you complete each task.

		Complete
~	Draw a squiggly line under the sentence that tells what Rebecca practiced on her way to school.	☐
—	Underline the sentence that tells why Rebecca was so thirsty that day.	☐
★	Draw a star next to the sentences that tell why Sam Simpson was known as "Seesaw."	☐
◢	Highlight the sentence that describes the look Miss Dearborn gave Rebecca when she asked to get a drink a third time.	☐
✖	Make an X next to the paragraph that describes what the schoolhouse was like inside.	☐
◯	Circle the paragraph that describes Rebecca's walk to school.	☐
[ ]	Draw brackets around the sentences that tell how Rebecca felt about being punished along with Sam.	☐
☐	Draw a box around the name of a saltwater fish.	☐
?	Write a question mark beside any words or sentences you don't understand.	☐

Name: _____

Apply Vocabulary

Use a word from the word box to complete each sentence.

Word Box

blackboard	conduct	exact	platform
punish	scholar	subject	uncomfortable

1. Some students sat on _____ wooden benches.

2. The teacher asked a boy to erase the lesson on the _____.

3. It is a rule of good _____ to raise your hand before speaking.

4. What is the _____ of the poem you are learning?

5. The young _____ answered the question correctly.

6. The teacher would _____ those who did not work quietly.

7. The teacher stood on a _____ so everyone could see her.

8. Rebecca counted the _____ number of books needed for the class.

Understanding Fiction: Classic Literature

A **classic literature** story is thought to be one of the best ever written. Some words in a classic story may sound old-fashioned to us today. Some classic stories tell us about life in times long ago.

Write your answers to the questions about the classic literature story.

1. Some words in a classic story are not used as often today. What word did the author use instead of "students"?

   _____

2. An author can show us what life was like long ago. For example, how did the scholars in Rebecca's school get a drink of water?

   _____

   _____

   _____

3. Which of these tell you that Rebecca's school was different from schools today?
   - ○ there was a pot-bellied stove
   - ○ there was one door for boys, one door for girls
   - ○ there were swings and slides
   - ○ there were blackboards
   - ○ there was a water pail and dipper
   - ○ there were wooden desks and benches
   - ○ there was only one teacher
   - ○ there were windows

4. Rebecca walked a mile to school. Which of these did she like to do along the way?
   - ○ startle the frogs
   - ○ wave away the cows
   - ○ fish for mackerel
   - ○ say her poem
   - ○ take a shortcut
   - ○ sing "The Old Oaken Bucket"
   - ○ jump from stone to stone
   - ○ swing her dinner pail

Name: _____

Literary Analysis: Character

When you think about a **character**, it helps you better understand that character. You can get to know the character by thinking about the following:

- what a character does
- what a character thinks
- what a character says
- how the author describes a character

Write your answers to the questions about the characters.

1. An author can show us how a character feels by the person's actions. List three things Miss Dearborn did that show how she felt.

   _____

   _____

   _____

2. Write one thing Rebecca thought that tells how she was feeling.

   _____

   _____

3. List three things the author wrote about Sam Simpson that helped you know more about him.

   _____

   _____

   _____

   _____

   _____

   _____

Answer Questions

Use information from the story to answer each question.

1. Rebecca went to _____.
   - Ⓐ a school in another town
   - Ⓑ a one-room schoolhouse
   - Ⓒ an old oaken school
   - Ⓓ a large school with many classrooms

2. In Rebecca's school, you would find _____.
   - Ⓐ computers
   - Ⓑ a drinking fountain
   - Ⓒ whiteboards and markers
   - Ⓓ a pail of water

3. Miss Dearborn raised her eyebrows because _____.
   - Ⓐ she was being silly
   - Ⓑ Rebecca wanted to sit near the window
   - Ⓒ Rebecca had asked for too many drinks
   - Ⓓ she didn't like salt mackerel

4. Why did Miss Dearborn punish Rebecca?

   _____

   _____

5. Why did the scholars want to sit in the back of the class?

   _____

   _____

Reading Literary Text • EMC 3213 • © Evan-Moor Corp.

Narrative Writing

Write a story about a scholar who goes to school in a one-room schoolhouse. Set your story in the past. Show by your character's actions if he or she is a good or bad scholar. Use details and vocabulary words from "Rebecca's School Day." Write a title for your story.

_____

_____

_____

_____

_____

_____

_____

_____

_____

_____

_____

_____

_____

_____

_____

LEVEL **N**

Never Kick a Slipper at the Moon, adapted from *Rootabaga Stories*
by Carl Sandburg
Fairy Tale

Lesson Objectives

Genre: Fairy Tale	Students will understand that a fairy tale is a make-believe story with magical events that may take place in an imaginary place.
Literary Analysis: Setting	Students will understand that the setting is where the story takes place and that a fairy tale may have a make-believe setting and a made-up name.
Narrative Writing: Dialogue	Students will write a dialogue to demonstrate understanding of the story's main idea.

Lesson Preparation

Reproduce and distribute to each student one copy of the story pages (pp. 65–66), the dictionary page (p. 67), and the activity pages (pp. 68–73).

Read and Learn		PAGE
1	Read Aloud the Fairy Tale	**65–66**
2	Introduce the Vocabulary *Dictionary*	**67**
3	Students Read the Fairy Tale	**65–66**
Analyze and Discuss		
4	*Read Closely*	**68**
5	*Close Reading Discussion*	**64**
Learn and Apply		
6	*Apply Vocabulary*	**69**
7	*Understanding Fiction: Fairy Tale*	**70**
8	*Literary Analysis: Setting*	**71**
Respond		
9	*Answer Questions*	**72**
10	*Narrative Writing* Don't Kick That Slipper!	**73**

CCSS: RL 3.1, 3.7, 3.10 **W** 3.3 **SL** 3.1, 3.1.a, 3.2

1 Read Aloud the Fairy Tale

Read aloud *Never Kick a Slipper at the Moon*. Have students follow along silently as you read.

2 Introduce the Vocabulary: Dictionary

Topic Vocabulary
Read aloud the words and definitions. Point out that a *dancing slipper* is a special shoe worn by dancers. Explain that both the *one-step* and the *two-step* are types of ballroom dances. Discuss definitions and usage as needed.

Academic Vocabulary
Read aloud the words and definitions. Explain that the word *stumble* means "to lose one's balance or trip." Point out that it contains the word *tumble*, but *tumble* has a different meaning (to fall helplessly). Discuss definitions and usage as needed.

3 Students Read the Fairy Tale

Have students read the fairy tale independently, with a partner, or in small groups. After students read, guide a discussion about the story.

4 Read Closely

Explain to students that this activity will help them locate important information in the story. Encourage students to mark any additional details they think are important.

5 Close Reading Discussion

Use the questions on the following page to guide students in discussing the fairy tale. Explain that close reading will help them notice important parts of the story. Encourage students to refer to the story as needed.

6 Apply Vocabulary

Guide students in completing the activity. Have students refer to the unit dictionary as needed.

7 Understanding Fiction: Fairy Tale

Read aloud the description of a fairy tale. Then guide students in completing the activity. Encourage them to refer to the story as needed.

8 Literary Analysis: Setting

Read aloud the description of how the setting affects a story. Then guide students in completing the activity, encouraging them to refer to the story as needed.

9 Answer Questions

To ensure reading comprehension, have students answer the text-dependent questions. Review the answers together.

You may wish to use this activity as a formative assessment to determine students' understanding of the text.

10 Narrative Writing: *Don't Kick That Slipper!*

Have students complete the writing activity independently, with a partner, or in small groups.

Close Reading Discussion

Ask students the following text-dependent questions and have them refer to the story as needed.

Questions	Sample Responses
How does the author show us that the girl was happy to see the moon when she went to the window?	*The girl sings to herself and kicks her foot toward the moon.*
What words were used to describe how the shoes walked or moved?	*"tramped," "marched," "stumbled," "softly," "clumping," "pigeon-toed," "glad and fast," "slow and sorry"*
The author, Carl Sandburg, called this story a fairy tale. A fairy tale has magic in it. What magical things happen in the story?	*Shoes and slippers walk by themselves in the middle of the night.* *A dancing slipper is kicked toward the moon and sticks to it.*
What does a dancing slipper moon look like?	*The ends of the moon look like the toe and heel of a dancer's foot.*
In what make-believe place do Mr. Wishes and his daughter live?	*Rootabaga Country*
What do you know about The Village of Cream Puffs?	*It is near Rootabaga Country; they have dances; there is a Dancing Slipper Moon in the sky.*
When did the shoes and slippers and boots walk out of the bedrooms and closets?	*in the middle of the night*
What do the illustrations tell you about the setting?	Answers will vary—Example: *Mr. Wishes is putting his daughter to bed. The slipper looks like the moon.*
The story says, "She saw a Dancing Slipper Moon. It was dancing far and high in the deep blue sea of the moon sky." Is this literal or nonliteral language? Explain your answer.	*This is nonliteral language, because a moon cannot dance and it is in the sky, not in the deep blue sea.*

Reading Literary Text • EMC 3213 • © Evan-Moor Corp.

Name: _____

Never Kick a Slipper at the Moon

Adapted from *Rootabaga Stories* by Carl Sandburg

When a girl is growing up in the Rootabaga Country, she learns some things to do and some things *not* to do, especially if her father is Mr. Wishes.

"Never kick a slipper at the moon if it is the time for the Dancing Slipper Moon. It is when the slim early moon looks like the toe and the heel of a dancer's foot," said Mr. Wishes to his daughter.

"Why?" she asked him.

"Because your slipper will go straight up, on and on to the moon. It will fasten itself on the moon as if the moon is a foot ready for dancing," said Mr. Wishes.

"How do you know?" asked his daughter.

"Well, let's see," said Mr. Wishes. "A long time ago in a village nearby, a secret word was passed around to all the shoes in the bedrooms and closets.

The secret was: *Tonight all the shoes and the slippers and the boots of the world are going walking without any feet in them!*

In the middle of the night, when the people in their beds were sleeping, the shoes and the slippers and the boots walked out of the bedrooms and closets. They walked along sidewalks and streets, down stairways, and along hallways.

They tramped and marched and stumbled.

Some walked softly just like people do. Some walked clumping and clumping. Some turned their toes in and walked pigeon-toed. Some ran glad and fast. Some lagged slow and sorry.

A little girl in the Village of Cream Puffs came home from a dance that night. And she was tired from dancing round dances and square dances. She was tired from dancing one-steps and two-steps and toe dances and toe-and-heel dances. She was so tired that she took off only one slipper and tumbled onto her bed. She went to sleep with one slipper on.

She woke up in the morning when it was yet dark. And she went to the window and looked up in the sky. She saw a Dancing Slipper Moon. It was dancing far and high in the deep blue sea of the moon sky.

"Oh—what a moon—what a dancing slipper of a moon!" she sang to herself.

She opened the window, saying again, "Oh! What a moon!"

And she kicked her foot with the slipper on it toward the moon.

The slipper flew off and flew up and went on and on. It flew up and up in the moonshine.

It never came back, that slipper. It was never seen again. When they asked the girl about it, she said, "It slipped off my foot and went up and up. The last I saw of it, the slipper was going on straight to the moon."

"So *that's* why I should never kick a slipper at the moon," said Mr. Wishes' daughter.

"Yes," said Mr. Wishes. "Make sure you never kick a slipper at the moon when it looks like the toe and the heel of a dancer's foot."

Dictionary

Topic Vocabulary

dancing slipper
a shoe used for dancing

closet
a small room or cupboard used
for storing things

pigeon-toed
with toes or feet turned in

one-step
a dance with very quick steps

two-step
a round dance with sliding
steps

Academic Vocabulary

straight
without a bend or a curve

fasten
to tie or hold something
together

stumble
to walk in an unsteady way

lag
to move less quickly; to fall
behind

tumble
to fall in a helpless way

Write a sentence that includes at least one vocabulary word.

_____

_____

Name: _____

Read Closely

Check the box after you complete each task.

		Complete
~	Draw a squiggly line under the sentence that names the moon that looks like a dancer's foot.	☐
—	Underline the sentence that tells what secret was passed around to all the shoes.	☐
★	Draw a star next to the paragraph that tells what the shoes did in the middle of the night.	☐
🖍	Highlight any sentences that tell the different ways the shoes, slippers, and boots walked.	☐
▲	Draw a triangle next to the sentences that tell what happened when the girl kicked her foot toward the moon.	☐
✖	Make an X next to the paragraph that explains why the little girl was so tired that night.	☐
[ ]	Draw brackets around the words the girl said about her lost slipper.	☐
☐	Draw a box around the sentence that tells what the girl sang when she saw the moon in the deep blue sky.	☐
?	Write a question mark beside any words or sentences you don't understand.	☐

Apply Vocabulary

Use a word from the word box to complete each sentence.

Word Box

closet	fasten	lag	pigeon-toed
straight	stumble	tumble	two-step

1. Everyone made a circle and danced the _____.

2. The slippers danced out of the _____.

3. Her slipper went _____ up to the moon.

4. The tired little dancer will _____ into bed.

5. Can a dancing slipper _____ itself to the moon?

6. The slower dancers always _____ behind us.

7. The tired dancers will _____ out of the room.

8. Turn your toes in and walk _____.

Name: _____

Understanding Fiction: Fairy Tale

A **fairy tale** is a make-believe story that is told as if it were true. A fairy tale may have magic in it. Many fairy tales have happy endings.

Write your answers to the questions about the fairy tale.

1. Who tells the story of the Dancing Slipper Moon?

   _____

2. Like most fathers do, Mr. Wishes tells his daughter what to do and what not to do. What does he tell her?

   _____

   _____

3. What magical thing happened one night while people were asleep?

   _____

   _____

   _____

4. What magical thing happened at the end of the story?

   _____

   _____

   _____

5. Did this fairy tale have a happy ending? Explain why or why not.

   _____

   _____

Literary Analysis: Setting

The **setting** is where a story takes place. The setting can make the story seem real or make-believe. In a make-believe place, magical things may happen. Ask yourself:

- Does the story take place in a real place?
- Does the story take place in a make-believe place with a made-up name?

Write your answers to the questions about the setting.

1. Where do Mr. Wishes and his daughter live?

   _____

2. The girl who kicked her slipper to the moon lives in the Village of Cream Puffs. What things make this village seem make-believe? Explain your answer.

   _____

   _____

   _____

3. What things make the Village of Cream Puffs seem real? Explain your answer.

   _____

   _____

   _____

4. Do the names of places in the story seem real or make-believe? Explain why.

   _____

   _____

Name: _____

Answer Questions

Use information from the fairy tale to answer each question.

1. The Dancing Slipper Moon is _____.
   - Ⓐ a slipper
   - Ⓑ a real place
   - Ⓒ make-believe
   - Ⓓ in the deep blue sea

2. Mr. Wishes tells his daughter _____.
   - Ⓐ a bedtime story
   - Ⓑ how to dance a two-step
   - Ⓒ why the moon changes
   - Ⓓ to put her shoes in the closet

3. All the shoes, slippers, and boots _____.
   - Ⓐ wished to go to the moon
   - Ⓑ were never seen again
   - Ⓒ were sleeping
   - Ⓓ walked out of the closets

4. Why did the girl kick her dancing slipper at the moon?

   _____

   _____

5. Mr. Wishes says to never kick a slipper at the moon. Why?

   _____

   _____

   _____

Narrative Writing

Pretend that your friend wants to kick her slipper at the moon. But you know that it is a Dancing Slipper Moon, so you need to warn her what will happen. Write a dialogue telling what you will say to warn her. Also write what she says to you in reply.

Don't Kick That Slipper!

_____

_____

_____

_____

_____

_____

_____

_____

_____

_____

_____

_____

_____

_____

_____

Lesson Objectives

Genre: Tall Tale	Students will understand that a tall tale is a story that stretches the truth, but it is told as if it were true and that the hero is sometimes based on a real person.
Literary Analysis: Character	Students will learn that characters in a tall tale are larger than life and that the words and actions of the characters help the reader better understand them.
Literary Response: Opinion	Students will write an opinion about the main character, provide reasons for their opinion, and use words such as *because, therefore, since,* and *for example.*

Lesson Preparation

Reproduce and distribute to each student one copy of the story pages (pp. 77–78), the dictionary page (p. 79), and the activity pages (pp. 80–85).

Read and Learn | PAGE
1 Read Aloud the Tall Tale | **77–78**
2 Introduce the Vocabulary *Dictionary* | **79**
3 Students Read the Tall Tale | **77–78**

Analyze and Discuss
4 *Read Closely* | **80**
5 *Close Reading Discussion* | **76**

Learn and Apply
6 *Apply Vocabulary* | **81**
7 *Understanding Fiction: Tall Tale* | **82**
8 *Literary Analysis: Character* | **83**

Respond
9 *Answer Questions* | **84**
10 *Literary Response* Davy Crockett | **85**

CCSS: **RL** 3.1, 3.2, 3.3, 3.4, 3.6, 3.7, 3.10   **W** 3.1   **SL** 3.1, 3.1.a, 3.2

1 Read Aloud the Tall Tale

Read aloud *Davy Crockett Escapes a Tornado.* Have students follow along silently as you read.

2 Introduce the Vocabulary: Dictionary

Topic Vocabulary
Read aloud the words and definitions. Point out that *bolt* has more than one meaning. In this story, it is a flash of lightning. It can also mean "to dash off or run away suddenly." Discuss definitions and usage as needed.

Academic Vocabulary
Read aloud the words and definitions. Explain that *mighty* is made from the word *might*, which means "great power or strength." Someone *mighty* has great strength. For the word *squirm*, ask a volunteer to demonstrate how to squirm in his or her seat. Discuss definitions and usage as needed.

3 Students Read the Tall Tale

Have students read the tall tale independently, with a partner, or in small groups. After students read, guide a discussion about the story.

4 Read Closely

Explain to students that this activity will help them locate important information in the story. Encourage students to mark any additional details they think are important.

5 Close Reading Discussion

Use the questions on the following page to guide students in discussing the tall tale. Explain that close reading will help them notice important parts of the story. Encourage students to refer to the story as needed.

6 Apply Vocabulary

Guide students in completing the activity. Have students refer to the unit dictionary as needed.

7 Understanding Fiction: Tall Tale

Read aloud the description of a tall tale. Then guide students in completing the activity. Encourage them to refer to the story as needed.

8 Literary Analysis: Character

Read aloud the description of how a character's words and actions help us to understand the character. Then guide students in completing the activity, encouraging them to refer to the story as needed.

9 Answer Questions

To ensure reading comprehension, have students answer the text-dependent questions. Review the answers together.

You may wish to use this activity as a formative assessment to determine students' understanding of the text.

10 Literary Response: *Davy Crockett*

Have students complete the writing activity independently, with a partner, or in small groups.

Close Reading Discussion

Ask students the following text-dependent questions and have them refer to the story as needed.

Questions	Sample Responses
In a tall tale, the main character is larger than life. Davy Crockett was stronger and braver than the average person. What did he say he could do?	*He said he could wrestle a bear and tame an alligator. He said he could show folks how to run the country.*
Who is telling this story?	*Davy Crockett is telling the story.*
Is the story told in the first person or the third person?	*The story is told in the first person.*
Does this tall tale include nonliteral language? If yes, provide examples from the story.	*Yes, there are many examples of nonliteral language in the story.* *Examples: "…our voices were about as loud as low thunder"; "Why, it roared like the very voice of Niagara Falls"; "The water began to squirm about like a stirred-up punch bowl"; "Then came a roar that would have made old Niagara sound like a kitten."*
Explain the meaning of one of the phrases or sentences.	Answers will vary.
Were Ben and Davy good friends? Explain your answer.	*Yes, they seemed like good friends because they spent time together talking and they cooperated with each other.*
What did Davy use to make the lightning bolt go faster?	*He used a bottle of rattlesnake oil.*
Why did they want to go faster?	*They wanted to leave the tornado behind them.*
What is Niagara Falls? How do you know from the story?	*a huge waterfall* *"It was so loud that it sounded like the pounding of a huge waterfall. Why, it roared like the very voice of Niagara Falls."*
What does the first picture help you understand about the setting of the story?	Answers will vary.
What does the second picture tell you about how the characters felt?	*Davy Crockett enjoyed the ride; Ben Hardin was frightened.*

Name: _____

Davy Crockett Escapes a Tornado

Adapted from Davy Crockett's *1846 Almanac*

Everyone has heard about the all-sweeping, all-smashing tornado that happened at Natchez. But they have never heard the facts about how Ben Hardin and I escaped from it. So I'll just tell you how it was.

You see, Ben Hardin and I were sitting on a steamboat on the mighty Mississippi River. We were talking about the way things were going in the country. As it always happens, our voices were about as loud as low thunder.

"By gosh, I should go to Washington myself," I rumbled.

"Davy, you sure could set things right there," agreed Ben.

"Why, I can wrestle a bear and tame an alligator. It's for sure I could show those folks how to run the country," I boomed.

All of a sudden, we heard a far-off roar! It was so loud that it sounded like the pounding of a huge waterfall. Why, it roared like the very voice of Niagara Falls.

"Hello, that's a storm a-coming," said the steamboat captain.

"No, it's just another steamboat," said Ben.

"Bah! It's only the echo of our own voices," says I.

But the noise grew bigger and bigger. The water began to squirm about like a stirred-up punch bowl. The boats on the river began rocking like a seesaw. Even I couldn't hold them still. Then came a roar that would have made old Niagara sound like a kitten. The trees walked out by their roots and danced about. Houses came apart. Lightning and thunder crashed closer and closer.

Ben and I thought the storm was just beginning, and it was time to be off. We were in luck. A stray streak of lightning came passing along right then. Just as it did, I grabbed it. Next, I sprang up onto that lightning bolt and started to ride. I rode it like a wild horse.

"Hop on, Ben!" I shouted.

"I'm right behind you, Davy!" called Ben.

Ben jumped on close behind me and held on to my hair. I took a bottle of rattlesnake oil out of my pocket. I used it to grease that lightning bolt and make it go faster. It worked. We streaked away as fast as greased lightning. Ben and I left the tornado behind. We were a sight to see!

And that's the true story of how Ben Hardin and I escaped the all-sweeping, all-smashing tornado at Natchez.

Dictionary

Topic Vocabulary

tornado
a whirling wind with a funnel-shaped cloud that destroys things in its path

Washington
Washington, D.C., the capital of the United States, where the laws of the country are made

Niagara Falls
a large waterfall on the border between the U.S. and Canada

captain
a person in charge of a ship

bolt
a flash of lightning

Academic Vocabulary

escape
to get out and away from something

mighty
very great and powerful

rumble
to make a long, deep, heavy sound

wrestle
to try to force a person to the ground

squirm
to wriggle and twist

stray
to move away from the place where you should be

grease
an oily substance that can be rubbed on something

Write a sentence that includes at least one vocabulary word.

_____

_____

Name: _____

Read Closely

Check the box after you complete each task.

		Complete
~	Draw a squiggly line under the sentence that shows that Davy Crockett was a strong and brave hunter.	☐
—	Read the paragraph that begins, "But the noise grew bigger and bigger." Underline the sentence that describes the sound of the tornado.	☐
★	Draw a star next to the sentence that describes how Davy Crockett used a bottle of rattlesnake oil.	☐
✎	Highlight the sentence that tells what Davy Crockett said he could do in Washington.	☐
▲	Draw a triangle next to the sentence that states this is a true story.	☐
✖	Make an X next to the paragraph that says Davy himself will tell the facts about his escape from a tornado.	☐
[ ]	Draw brackets around the sentence that tells what happened right when Davy and Ben decided it was time to go.	☐
☐	Draw a box around the sentence that tells what Ben said when Davy told him to hop onto the lightning bolt.	☐
?	Write a question mark beside any words or sentences you don't understand.	☐

Apply Vocabulary

Use a word from the word box to complete each sentence.

Word Box

bolt	captain	escape	mighty
Niagara Falls	rumble	squirm	wrestle

1. Davy Crockett was strong enough to _____ a bear.

2. We heard the _____ of thunder in the distance.

3. There was a _____ storm that day.

4. Boats rocked when the water began to _____.

5. The ship's _____ said that a storm was coming.

6. A _____ of lightning flashed across the sky.

7. The noise was as loud as _____.

8. Davy and Ben thought it was time to _____.

Understanding Fiction: Tall Tale

An American **tall tale** is an old story about a larger-than-life character that is a hero. A hero is sometimes based on a real person. The story is told as if it were true. However, a tall tale stretches the truth.

Write your answers to the questions about the tall tale.

1. Davy Crockett was a real person. He was alive when America was a young country. Who tells this story?

   _____

2. Davy Crockett is a larger-than-life character. List two things he could do that show how strong and brave he was.

   _____

   _____

3. This story stretches the truth. How did Davy Crockett and Ben Hardin escape the tornado?

   _____

   _____

4. Mark all the things that make this story a tall tale.
   ○ A person cannot ride a lightning bolt.
   ○ Davy Crockett was a real person.
   ○ Davy Crockett and Ben Hardin were friends.
   ○ Davy greased a lightning bolt with rattlesnake oil.

Literary Analysis: Character

When you think about what a **character** says and does, it helps you to better understand that character. You can also think about the following:

- what the character thinks
- how the character changes
- how the author describes the character
- the character's relationships with others

Write your answers to the questions about the main character.

1. Do you think Davy Crockett was a quiet person or a loud person? Give an example from the story.

   _____

   _____

2. How do you know that Davy Crockett didn't like the way folks in Washington ran the country? Write his words from the story.

   _____

   _____

3. What action words are used to describe what Davy Crockett did?

   _____

   _____

   _____

4. Davy said that he could wrestle a bear and tame an alligator. What does that tell you about Davy?

   _____

   _____

Name: _____

Answer Questions

Use information from the tall tale to answer each question.

1. The story "Davy Crockett Escapes a Tornado" is told by _____.
   - Ⓐ a person who saw it happen
   - Ⓑ Ben Hardin
   - Ⓒ a steamboat captain
   - Ⓓ Davy himself

2. The story takes place _____.
   - Ⓐ in a make-believe place
   - Ⓑ today at Natchez
   - Ⓒ long ago on the Mississippi River
   - Ⓓ at Niagara Falls

3. Davy Crockett _____.
   - Ⓐ said he rode a lightning bolt
   - Ⓑ was a steamboat captain
   - Ⓒ didn't like to talk about himself
   - Ⓓ was afraid of lightning

4. How did Davy describe the sound of the tornado?

   _____

   _____

5. The saying "as fast as greased lightning" describes something that moves very fast. How was that idea used in this story?

   _____

   _____

Literary Response

If you had lived in Davy Crockett's time, would you have liked having him for a friend? Write an opinion that tells why or why not. Use words such as *because, therefore, since,* and *for example.*

Davy Crockett

_____

_____

_____

_____

_____

_____

_____

_____

_____

_____

_____

_____

_____

Lesson Objectives

Genre: Poetry Students will understand that a poem tells about an idea, a feeling, or an event and recognize that some poems are songs.

Literary Analysis: Language of Poetry Students will learn that poems and songs can have rhyme and repetition and use onomatopoeia.

Narrative Writing: Writing Poetry Students will compose a poem about a present-day Thanksgiving.

Lesson Preparation

Reproduce and distribute to each student one copy of the poem pages (pp. 89–90), the dictionary page (p. 91), and the activity pages (pp. 92–97).

Read and Learn	PAGE
1 Read Aloud the Poem	**89–90**
2 Introduce the Vocabulary *Dictionary*	**91**
3 Students Read the Poem	**90–91**
Analyze and Discuss	
4 *Read Closely*	**92**
5 *Close Reading Discussion*	**88**
Learn and Apply	
6 *Apply Vocabulary*	**93**
7 *Understanding Poetry*	**94**
8 *Literary Analysis: Language of Poetry*	**95**
Respond	
9 *Answer Questions*	**96**
10 *Narrative Writing* A Thanksgiving Day Poem	**97**

CCSS: RL 3.1, 3.5, 3.7, 3.10   W 3.3   SL 3.1, 3.1.a, 3.2

1 Read Aloud the Poem

Read aloud *The New-England Boy's Song About Thanksgiving Day*. Have students follow along silently as you read. Explain that some poems are actually songs. Then sing the song together.

2 Introduce the Vocabulary: Dictionary

Topic Vocabulary

Read aloud the words and definitions. Point out that the words *dapple grey* mean "a spotted gray horse." Explain that *grey* is another way to spell the color gray. Discuss definitions and usage as needed.

Academic Vocabulary

Read aloud the words and definitions. Explain that *hark* means "to listen." Point out that *pow* is an old-fashioned word for *head* and that it is rarely used today.

3 Students Read the Poem

Have students read the poem independently, with a partner, or in small groups. Then guide a discussion about the poem.

4 Read Closely

Explain to students that this activity will help them locate important details in the poem. Encourage students to mark any additional details they think are important.

5 Close Reading Discussion

Use the questions on the following page to guide students in discussing the poem. Explain that close reading will help them notice important parts of the poem. Encourage students to refer to the poem as needed.

6 Apply Vocabulary

Guide students in completing the activity. Have students refer to the unit dictionary as needed.

7 Understanding Poetry

Read aloud the description of a poem. Then guide students in completing the activity. Encourage them to refer to the poem as needed.

8 Literary Analysis: Language of Poetry

Read aloud the description of language of poetry. Then guide students in completing the activity, encouraging them to refer to the poem as needed.

9 Answer Questions

To ensure reading comprehension, have students answer the text-dependent questions. Review the answers together.

You may wish to use this activity as a formative assessment to determine students' understanding of the poem.

10 Narrative Writing: *A Thanksgiving Day Poem*

Have students complete the writing activity independently, with a partner, or in small groups.

Close Reading Discussion

Ask students the following text-dependent questions and have them refer to the poem as needed.

Questions	Sample Responses
How does each verse begin?	*"Over the river, and through the wood"*
This song is made up of 12 verses. Each verse has a number. In verse 1, what does the horse know?	*"The horse knows the way, / To carry the sleigh."*
In verse 5, what sound do the bells make?	*"Ting a ling ding"*
In verse 3, how cold is the wind?	*"It stings the toes, / And bites the nose"*
Is this literal or nonliteral language? Explain why.	*This is nonliteral language. The wind is not a person or an animal that can sting or bite.*
In verse 6, what does "upset" mean?	**Upset** *means "turned over."*
What words in the verse helped you figure it out?	*"Into a bank of snow."*
In verse 9, how does the boy feel about waiting?	*"We seem to go / Extremely slow, / It is so hard to wait."*
From reading verse 12, what do you know about grandmother?	*She wears a cap. She has been baking.*
Does each verse tell you a little bit more about what is happening in the poem? Explain your answer.	Example: *Yes. The second verse says that they will not stop, and the third verse says that the wind is cold and makes them feel cold as they ride in the sleigh.*
Narrative poetry tells a story. Do you think this is narrative poetry? Explain your answer.	*Yes, because it tells the story of a family going to their grandparents' house for Thanksgiving Day.*
How do the illustrations help you better understand the setting of the poem and the phrase, "Over the river, and through the wood"?	Answers will vary.
Do the illustrations help you understand more about the people in the poem?	Answers will vary.

Name: _____

The New-England Boy's Song About Thanksgiving Day

by Lydia Maria Child

1 Over the river, and through the wood,
To grandfather's house we go;
The horse knows the way,
To carry the sleigh,
Through the white and drifted snow.

2 Over the river, and through the wood,
To grandfather's house away!
We would not stop
For doll or top,
For 'tis Thanksgiving Day.

3 Over the river, and through the wood,
Oh, how the wind does blow!
It stings the toes,
And bites the nose,
As over the ground we go.

4 Over the river, and through the wood,
With a clear blue winter sky,
The dogs do bark,
And children hark,
As we go jingling by.

5 Over the river, and through the wood,
To have a first-rate play—
Hear the bells ring
Ting a ling ding,
Hurra for Thanksgiving Day!

⁶ Over the river, and through the wood—
No matter for winds that blow;
Or if we get
The sleigh upset,
Into a bank of snow.

⁷ Over the river, and through the wood,
To see little John and Ann;
We will kiss them all,
And play snow-ball,
And stay as long as we can.

⁸ Over the river, and through the wood,
Trot fast, my dapple grey!
Spring over the ground,
Like a hunting hound,
For 'tis Thanksgiving Day!

⁹ Over the river, and through the wood,
And straight through the barn-yard gate;
We seem to go
Extremely slow,
It is so hard to wait.

¹⁰ Over the river, and through the wood,
Old Jowler hears our bells;
He shakes his pow,
With a loud bow-wow,
And thus the news he tells.

¹¹ Over the river, and through the wood—
When grandmother sees us come,
She will say, Oh dear,
The children are here,
Bring a pie for every one.

¹² Over the river, and through the wood—
Now grandmother's cap I spy!
Hurra for the fun!
Is the pudding done?
Hurra for the pumpkin pie!

Name: _____

Dictionary

Topic Vocabulary

sleigh
a carriage mounted on runners and used on snow or ice

drift
snow piled up by the wind

upset
tipped over

dapple grey
a gray horse marked with darker gray spots

Academic Vocabulary

'tis
it is

hark
to listen

first-rate
excellent; of the highest class

extremely
much more or much less than usual

pow
an old-fashioned word for *head*

spy
to see

Write a sentence that includes at least one vocabulary word.

_____

_____

Name: _____

Read Closely

Check the box after you complete each task.

		Complete
~	This song has 12 verses. In verse 1, what does the horse know? Draw a squiggly line under the words that tell you.	☐
—	Underline the words in verse 5 that tell what sound the bells make.	☐
★	Draw a star next to the lines that tell what grandmother will say when she sees them coming.	☐
🖊	Highlight the words in verse 3 that tell how cold the wind is.	☐
✖	Make an X next to the verse that tells who will play in the snow.	☐
◯	Circle the words that are repeated at the beginning of each verse.	☐
[ ]	Draw brackets around the words in verse 9 that tell how the boy feels about waiting.	☐
☐	Draw a box around the line that tells how the boy feels about his grandmother's pie.	☐
?	Write a question mark beside any words or sentences you don't understand.	☐

Name: _____

Apply Vocabulary

Use a word from the word box to complete each sentence.

Word Box			
dapple grey	drift	extremely	first-rate
sleigh	spy	'Tis	upset

1. There was a tall _____ of snow by the door.

2. I _____ children playing in the snow down the street.

3. We heard the jingle of _____ bells getting closer.

4. We made a _____ snowman in the front yard.

5. The blowing wind felt _____ cold on my nose.

6. The hounds ran into the room and _____ the food table.

7. Her horse is the _____ in the stable.

8. _____ time for the pumpkin pie!

Understanding Poetry

A **poem** is a group of words that tell about an idea, a feeling, or an event. Some poems are songs.

Write your answers to the questions about the poem.

1. This poem gives us a look at life long ago in New England. Write one example of how we know the poem took place long ago.

   _____

   _____

2. Write the lines of the poem that tell what grandmother will say.

   _____

   _____

   _____

   _____

3. How does Old Jowler tell the news?

   _____

   _____

4. What event is this poem about?

   _____

   _____

Literary Analysis: Language of Poetry

Poetry uses **language** that makes us think about and feel and see things differently. Here are some ways that language may be used in a poem or a song:

- rhyme
- onomatopoeia
- repetition
- action words

Write your answers to the questions about the language in the poem.

1. This poem has rhyming word pairs. For example, *The horse knows the **way*** / *To carry the **sleigh***. Write two more lines that have a rhyming word pair. Then circle the words that rhyme.

   _____

   _____

2. This poem uses onomatopoeia, or words for sounds. Write the words that were used for a dog barking and bells ringing.

   _____

   _____

3. List action words from verse 3 that describe the wind.

   _____

   _____

4. Which line of the poem is repeated over and over?

   _____

   _____

Answer Questions

Use your reading of the poem to answer each question.

1. This poem is _____.
   - Ⓐ a happy song
   - Ⓑ about the Fourth of July
   - Ⓒ by an unknown author
   - Ⓓ a sad song

2. The line "Trot fast, my dapple grey!" is probably about _____.
   - Ⓐ catching a hunting hound
   - Ⓑ being lost in the woods
   - Ⓒ riding a dapple grey horse
   - Ⓓ a gray horse trotting fast

3. _____ knows the way to grandfather's house.
   - Ⓐ Old Jowler
   - Ⓑ The horse
   - Ⓒ The sleigh
   - Ⓓ The sleigh driver

4. How would you describe the time and place of this poem?

   _____

   _____

   _____

5. How does the poem describe the way to grandfather's house?

   _____

   _____

Name: _____

Narrative Writing

"The New-England Boy's Song About Thanksgiving Day" takes place long ago. Write a short poem about a family that travels somewhere to have Thanksgiving dinner. Your poem does not have to rhyme. Choose one of the ideas below or make up your own:

- a plane ride to see Grandma
- a family bike ride
- a train ride to the city

A Thanksgiving Day Poem

_____

_____

_____

_____

_____

_____

_____

_____

_____

_____

_____

nch with Diego
Historical Fiction

sson Objectives

Genre: Historical Fiction	Students will understand that historical fiction is a story that takes place in the past. Some of the characters may be real people from history, but the story is not true.
Literary Analysis: Plot	Students will understand that the plot is the order of events in a story. The actions of the characters move the story along from beginning to middle to ending.
Literary Response: Summary	Students will write a summary of the main events in the story.

Lesson Preparation

Reproduce and distribute to each student one copy of the story pages (pp. 101–102), the dictionary page (p. 103), and the activity pages (pp. 104–109).

Read and Learn

		PAGE
1	Read Aloud the Story	**101–102**
2	Introduce the Vocabulary *Dictionary*	**103**
3	Students Read the Story	**101–102**

Analyze and Discuss

4	*Read Closely*	**104**
5	*Close Reading Discussion*	**100**

Learn and Apply

6	*Apply Vocabulary*	**105**
7	*Understanding Fiction: Historical Fiction*	**106**
8	*Literary Analysis: Plot*	**107**

Respond

9	*Answer Questions*	**108**
10	*Literary Response* A Summary of "Lunch with Diego"	**109**

CCSS: **RL** 3.1, 3.7, 3.10   **W** 3.2   **SL** 3.1, 3.1.a, 3.2

1 Read Aloud the Story

Read aloud *Lunch with Diego.* Have students follow along silently as you read.

2 Introduce the Vocabulary: Dictionary

Topic Vocabulary
Read aloud the words and definitions. Explain that the word *fresco* comes from an Italian word meaning "fresh." A fresco is a painting done on fresh plaster. Point out that *automobile* has two parts. *Auto* means "by itself." *Mobile* is an old-fashioned word for a moving vehicle. Together they mean "a vehicle that moves by itself." Discuss definitions and usage as needed.

Academic Vocabulary
Read aloud the words and definitions. Explain that in this story, *plant* means "a place where automobiles are manufactured." Point out that a *master* is an expert, or a person who is very skilled in a particular art or trade. Discuss definitions and usage as needed.

3 Students Read the Story

Have students read the story independently, with a partner, or in small groups. After students read, guide a discussion about the story.

4 Read Closely

Explain to students that this activity will help them locate important information in the story. Encourage students to mark any additional details they think are important.

5 Close Reading Discussion

Use the questions on the following page to guide students in discussing the story. Explain that close reading will help them notice important parts of the story. Encourage students to refer to the story as needed.

6 Apply Vocabulary

Guide students in completing the activity. Have students refer to the unit dictionary as needed.

7 Understanding Fiction: Historical Fiction

Read aloud the description of historical fiction. Then guide students in completing the activity. Encourage them to refer to the story as needed.

8 Literary Analysis: Plot

Read aloud the description of how the characters affect the plot. Then guide students in completing the activity, encouraging them to refer to the story as needed.

9 Answer Questions

To ensure reading comprehension, have students answer the text-dependent questions. Review the answers together.

You may wish to use this activity as a formative assessment to determine students' understanding of the text.

10 Literary Response: *A Summary of* "Lunch with Diego"

Have students complete the writing activity independently, with a partner, or in small groups.

Close Reading Discussion

Ask students the following text-dependent questions and have them refer to the story as needed.

Questions	Sample Responses
How real did the painting of giant machines seem to the boy? Which sentences in the story tell you this?	*It seemed very real and lifelike to him, as if he could almost hear the noise.* *"An automobile plant was coming to life on the walls. I could almost hear its noisy clatter."*
What did the boy mean when he said, "An automobile plant was coming to life on the walls."	Answers will vary.
Why did the boy especially like the art institute? Give more than one reason.	*Because he loved to draw and paint, and the institute was full of works of art. It was close to his school, so he could go there at lunchtime. Also, he got to see a master painter at work and meet him.*
How is a fresco made?	*A fresco is painted on wet plaster. When the plaster dries, the painting becomes part of the wall. A painter uses a scaffold to reach the high places first, and then works down the wall.*
What do you think Diego and Frida probably thought when they saw the sketch the boy had made of Frida? How do you know?	*They thought the boy was a good artist and wanted to encourage him. I know this because they stopped their work in order to tell him so.*
How do you know the Rivera frescoes are still special to the main character, even now that he is grown?	*He says he returns every now and then to visit them, and he still remembers watching the master at work.*
Did the illustrations help you better understand the characters in the story? If so, tell why.	Answers will vary.
Is the story told in the first person or the third person? How do you know?	*The story is told in the first person because the boy says, "I will always remember the time a famous artist came to my town."*
What sensory language was used in the story? What did the boy see?	Answers will vary—Example: *"The cloths were spattered with paint and plaster"; "Faces of many colors popped out at me."*

Name: _____

Lunch with Diego

I will always remember the time a famous artist came to my town. He was Diego Rivera, from Mexico. He left his mark not only on me but on America, too.

I grew up in Detroit, Michigan, in the 1930s. At that time, Detroit was well known for making automobiles. My school was in the city, not far from the Detroit Institute of Arts. This magical place was full of works of art. It was perfect for a kid like me who loved to draw and paint.

One day, my teacher, Miss Pickford, took our class to visit the Detroit Institute of Arts. The newspaper had said Diego Rivera would be there, painting frescoes on the walls of the garden court! Miss Pickford explained that frescoes were big paintings on wet plaster. As the plaster dried, the painting became part of the wall.

At the art institute, we poked our noses through the closed gate of the garden court. It was so messy and busy! Scaffolds were everywhere, with cloths placed under them. The cloths were spattered with paint and plaster. A colorful world was being created.

Diego Rivera was nowhere to be found. There was only an empty chair high up on a scaffold. Next to it was a table holding pots of paints and brushes. The painter had started painting at the ceiling, and was working down from there. Giant machines and twisting pipes filled the scene. Faces of many colors popped out at me. An automobile plant was coming to life on the walls. I could almost hear its noisy clatter. I knew I had to come back to see this amazing master at work!

The next day at lunchtime, I took my lunch, drawing pencils,

and notebook to the art institute. I peered through the closed garden court gate. There he was!

Diego Rivera was a big man wearing baggy pants. His work jacket was spattered with paint. Quickly, I took out my paper and pencils and began to sketch him at work. Before I knew it, it was time to rush back to school.

After that day, I returned to the garden court as often as I could. I would sit outside the gate and sketch. One day, someone new appeared on the scaffold. She was a beautiful dark-haired lady. She wore a long white dress with a red shawl wrapped around her. Her hair was braided and pinned up around her head. That day, I drew a picture of the beautiful lady. I slipped it under the gate before I dashed away.

The next day at lunchtime, the gate to the garden court was open. I quietly slipped in and found a place to sit on the fountain wall. I was sketching when suddenly I felt a hand on my shoulder. I turned to look into the eyes of the beautiful dark-haired lady.

"My husband tells me you always come here with your lunch,"

she stated. "And you are always working on something in that notebook of yours."

I was too surprised to speak.

"Diego, come here please," she called. The big man put down his brush and walked over to us, smiling.

"Let's see what is in that notebook," he said. He flipped through my notebook. "Hmm, a true artist. And that picture of my wife, Frida, was very good. Keep sketching!"

All I could do was nod. Diego Rivera and his wife, Frida Kahlo, walked off to continue the frescoes.

Today, the frescoes can still be seen at the Detroit Institute of Arts. Although I'm not a famous artist, I still enjoy sketching. I return every now and then to visit the Diego Rivera frescoes. And I remember watching the master at work.

Name: _____

Dictionary

Topic Vocabulary

automobile
a four-wheeled vehicle with
an engine; a car

institute
a museum

fresco
a mural painted on wet plaster

plaster
a mixture that hardens and is
used for coating walls

scaffold
a raised framework or platform
used by workers

sketch
to make a rough drawing

Academic Vocabulary

court
an open space with walls on
all sides

spatter
to splash or scatter drops

scene
a view of a place

plant
factory buildings used for
making things

master
a person who has a great
amount of skill in or knowledge
about something

fountain
a structure that spouts water,
used for decoration

Write a sentence that includes at least one vocabulary word.

_____

_____

Name: _____

Read Closely

Check the box after you complete each task.

		Complete
~	Draw a squiggly line under the sentences that describe what Diego Rivera looked like.	☐
—	Underline the sentence that tells what Detroit, Michigan, was known for producing.	☐
★	Draw a star next to the sentence that tells what Frida Kahlo wore.	☐
✐	Highlight the sentence that tells what the boy did when Diego Rivera said his picture was very good.	☐
▲	Draw a triangle next to the sentence that tells what can be seen today at the Detroit Institute of Arts.	☐
✖	Make an X next to the paragraph that tells what Diego Rivera said to the young artist.	☐
○	Circle the word that tells what kind of plant Diego Rivera was painting.	☐
[ ]	Draw brackets around the sentences that explain what frescoes are.	☐
?	Write a question mark beside any words or sentences you don't understand.	☐

Name: _____

Apply Vocabulary

Use a word from the word box to complete each sentence.

Word Box			
automobile	court	fountain	fresco
Institute	plant	scaffold	sketch

1. Water flowed from the tall _____ in the courtyard.

2. A _____ is painted on wet plaster.

3. The master painted an _____ factory scene.

4. It would be fun to visit the Detroit _____ of Arts.

5. He climbed a _____ to reach the high places.

6. I will _____ a picture of you at lunchtime.

7. She works in a _____ where automobiles are made.

8. The gate to the garden _____ was locked.

Understanding Fiction: Historical Fiction

Historical fiction is a story that takes place in the past. Although the story seems real, it is not true.

- The setting is a real place and time in history.
- Some of the characters are real people from history.
- Details about the time and place make the story come alive.

Write your answers to the questions about the historical fiction story.

1. During what time period does most of the story take place?

   _____

   _____

2. What type of work did many people do in Detroit, Michigan?

   _____

   _____

3. Which characters in the story were real people from history?

   _____

   _____

4. Mark each detail that describes Diego Rivera or Frida Kahlo.
   - ○ from Mexico
   - ○ wore a long white dress with a red shawl
   - ○ grew up in Detroit, Michigan
   - ○ a big man wearing baggy pants
   - ○ giant machines and twisting pipes
   - ○ a beautiful dark-haired lady
   - ○ an amazing master
   - ○ home of the automobile

Literary Analysis: Plot

> The **plot** is the order of events in a story. There is a beginning, middle, and ending. The characters move the plot along through their actions. Look for these things in the plot:
>
> - A problem starts at the beginning.
> - An uncertain feeling or a new character comes in the middle.
> - The problem is settled at the end of the story.

Write your answers to the questions about the plot.

1. At the beginning of the story, how did the boy first learn about Diego Rivera?

    _____

    _____

2. In the middle of the story, the boy went back to the garden court again and again. One day, he left one of his sketches. What was different the next day?

    _____

    _____

3. Frida Kahlo came into the story at a high point. What did she do that made her an important character in the story?

    _____

    _____

4. At the end of the story, we learn that the boy still sketches. What else does he do?

    _____

    _____

Answer Questions

Use information from the historical fiction story to answer each question.

1. In this story, Diego Rivera painted frescoes _____.
   - Ⓐ with the help of children
   - Ⓑ of workers and machines
   - Ⓒ in a school in Detroit
   - Ⓓ of his wife, Frida Kahlo

2. Every day, the boy went _____.
   - Ⓐ to art class
   - Ⓑ to watch Diego Rivera paint
   - Ⓒ with his teacher to the garden court
   - Ⓓ home for lunch

3. One day, the boy was able to _____.
   - Ⓐ paint a fresco
   - Ⓑ play in the fountain
   - Ⓒ meet the master artist
   - Ⓓ visit an automobile plant

4. What did the boy leave behind that led to his meeting Diego Rivera?

   _____

   _____

5. Explain why you think the boy did not speak to Diego or Frida.

   _____

   _____

   _____

Name: _____

Literary Response

Write a summary of the main events in the story and each character's actions.

A Summary of "Lunch with Diego"

_____

_____

_____

_____

_____

_____

_____

_____

_____

_____

_____

_____

_____

_____

_____

LEVEL P

Damon and Pythias
Greek Legend

Lesson Objectives

Genre: Legend
Students will understand that a legend is a story told through the ages and that it is based on a real event and has real people and places from history.

Literary Analysis: Plot
Students will understand that the plot is the order of events in the story and that a story has a beginning, a middle, and an ending.

Literary Response: Opinion
Students will write an opinion on the topic of friendship.

Lesson Preparation

Reproduce and distribute to each student one copy of the story pages (pp. 113–114), the dictionary page (p. 115), and the activity pages (pp. 116–121).

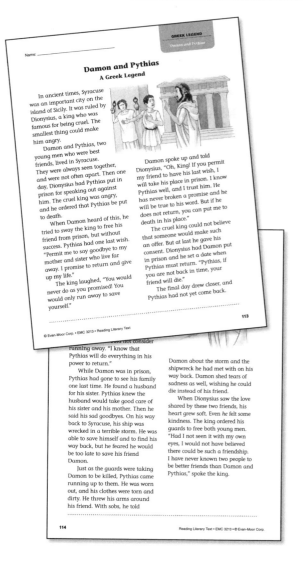

Read and Learn	PAGE
1 Read Aloud the Story	113–114
2 Introduce the Vocabulary *Dictionary*	115
3 Students Read the Story	113–114

Analyze and Discuss	
4 *Read Closely*	116
5 *Close Reading Discussion*	112

Learn and Apply	
6 *Apply Vocabulary*	117
7 *Understanding Fiction: Legend*	118
8 *Literary Analysis: Plot*	119

Respond	
9 *Answer Questions*	120
10 *Literary Response* Friendship	121

CCSS: **RL** 3.1, 3.2, 3.3, 3.4, 3.6, 3.7, 3.10   **W** 3.1   **SL** 3.1, 3.1.a, 3.2

1 Read Aloud the Story

Read aloud *Damon and Pythias*. Have students follow along silently as you read.

2 Introduce the Vocabulary: Dictionary

Topic Vocabulary

Read aloud the words and definitions. Point out that *ancient* describes something belonging to the early history of the world. For example, explain that a Greek legend is an *ancient* story told in Greece over a thousand years ago. Discuss definitions and usage as needed.

Academic Vocabulary

Read aloud the words and definitions. Explain that *consent* is used as a noun in this story, meaning "permission" as in this sentence: "The teacher gave his *consent* for us to work together." Discuss definitions and usage as needed.

3 Students Read the Story

Have students read the story independently, with a partner, or in small groups. After students read, guide a discussion about the story.

4 Read Closely

Explain to students that this activity will help them locate important information in the story. Encourage students to mark any additional details they think are important.

5 Close Reading Discussion

Use the questions on the following page to guide students in discussing the story. Explain that close reading will help them notice important parts of the story. Encourage students to refer to the story as needed.

6 Apply Vocabulary

Guide students in completing the activity. Have students refer to the unit dictionary as needed.

7 Understanding Fiction: Legend

Read aloud the description of a legend. Then guide students in completing the activity. Encourage them to refer to the story as needed.

8 Literary Analysis: Plot

Read aloud the description of how plot affects a story. Then guide students in completing the activity, encouraging them to refer to the story as needed.

9 Answer Questions

To ensure reading comprehension, have students answer the text-dependent questions. Review the answers together.

You may wish to use this activity as a formative assessment to determine students' understanding of the text.

10 Literary Response: *Friendship*

Have students complete the writing activity independently, with a partner, or in small groups.

Close Reading Discussion

Ask students the following text-dependent questions and have them refer to the story as needed.

Questions	Sample Responses
The setting is the time and place of a story. What is the setting of this legend? Read the sentences that describe the setting.	*This legend takes place in ancient times in the city of Syracuse on the island of Sicily.* *"In ancient times, Syracuse was an important city on the island of Sicily. It was ruled by Dionysius, a king who was famous for being cruel."*
What do the illustrations tell you about the setting?	Answers will vary.
The subject of the story is friendship. Who are the heroes of the story?	*Two friends, Damon and Pythias, are the heroes.*
What kind of ruler was Dionysius? Read aloud the sentences that tell you.	*Dionysius was a cruel king who put to death those who spoke against him.* *"It was ruled by Dionysius, a king who was famous for being cruel. The smallest thing could make him angry; …Dionysius had Pythias put in prison for speaking out against him. The cruel king was angry, and he ordered that Pythias be put to death."*
How do you know that Damon trusted Pythias to return?	*Because Damon offered to take his place in prison.*
In the middle of the story, we can't be sure if Pythias will return. Why?	Any of the following: *1) The final day was drawing closer, and Pythias had not yet come back; 2) Pythias is shipwrecked and he is afraid he will be too late; 3) The guards were taking Damon to be killed.*
Why did Dionysius change his mind? What did he do? Read aloud his words.	*He saw that Damon and Pythias had such a strong friendship. He freed both young men.* *"Had I not seen it with my own eyes, I would not have believed there could be such a friendship. I have never known two people to be better friends than Damon and Pythias."*
Damon said, "But if he does not return, you can put me to death in his place." Is this literal or nonliteral language? Explain your answer.	*This is literal language because Damon really means what he is saying. He believes his friend will never break a promise, so he offers to die, knowing his friend will return.*

Name: _____

Damon and Pythias
A Greek Legend

In ancient times, Syracuse was an important city on the island of Sicily. It was ruled by Dionysius, a king who was famous for being cruel. The smallest thing could make him angry.

Damon and Pythias, two young men who were best friends, lived in Syracuse. They were always seen together, and were not often apart. Then one day, Dionysius had Pythias put in prison for speaking out against him. The cruel king was angry, and he ordered that Pythias be put to death.

When Damon heard of this, he tried to sway the king to free his friend from prison, but without success. Pythias had one last wish. "Permit me to say goodbye to my mother and sister who live far away. I promise to return and give up my life."

The king laughed, "You would never do as you promised! You would only run away to save yourself."

Damon spoke up and told Dionysius, "Oh, King! If you permit my friend to have his last wish, I will take his place in prison. I know Pythias well, and I trust him. He has never broken a promise and he will be true to his word. But if he does not return, you can put me to death in his place."

The cruel king could not believe that someone would make such an offer. But at last he gave his consent. Dionysius had Damon put in prison and he set a date when Pythias must return. "Pythias, if you are not back in time, your friend will die."

The final day drew closer, and Pythias had not yet come back.

The king ordered his guards to watch Damon closely so he could not get away. But Damon trusted his friend and would not consider running away. "I know that Pythias will do everything in his power to return."

While Damon was in prison, Pythias had gone to see his family one last time. He found a husband for his sister. Pythias knew the husband would take good care of his sister and his mother. Then he said his sad goodbyes. On his way back to Syracuse, his ship was wrecked in a terrible storm. He was able to save himself and to find his way back, but he feared he would be too late to save his friend Damon.

Just as the guards were taking Damon to be killed, Pythias came running up to them. He was worn out, and his clothes were torn and dirty. He threw his arms around his friend. With sobs, he told Damon about the storm and the shipwreck he had met with on his way back. Damon shed tears of sadness as well, wishing he could die instead of his friend.

When Dionysius saw the love shared by these two friends, his heart grew soft. Even *he* felt some kindness. The king ordered his guards to free both young men. "Had I not seen it with my own eyes, I would not have believed there could be such a friendship. I have never known two people to be better friends than Damon and Pythias," spoke the king.

Reading Literary Text • EMC 3213 • © Evan-Moor Corp.

Name: _____

Dictionary

Topic Vocabulary

ancient
having to do with times long
past

cruel
liking to cause others pain
or suffering

prison
a place where people are locked
up for crimes they have done

permit
to allow

shipwreck
a ship destroyed by a storm

friendship
the state of being friends

Academic Vocabulary

apart
away from each other in time
or position

death
the end of life

sway
to change someone's thinking

consent
permission

final
coming at the end

wreck
to destroy by breaking up

Write a sentence that includes at least one vocabulary word.

_____

_____

Read Closely

Check the box after you complete each task.

		Complete
~	Draw a squiggly line under the sentence that tells what the king ordered after Pythias spoke out against him.	☐
—	Underline the sentence that describes the time and place of the story.	☐
★	Draw a star next to the sentence that explains Pythias's last wish.	☐
▱	Highlight the sentences that tell what Dionysius said after Pythias returned.	☐
▲	Draw a triangle next to the sentence that tells what happened to Pythias on his way back to save Damon.	☐
✖	Make an X next to the paragraph that tells what Damon said to the king that caused him to let Pythias say goodbye to his family.	☐
◯	Circle the words in the title that tell what type of fiction story this is.	☐
[ ]	Draw brackets around the sentence that tells why Damon was sad when his friend returned.	☐
?	Write a question mark beside any words or sentences you don't understand.	☐

Name: _____

Apply Vocabulary

Use a word from the word box to complete each sentence.

Word Box			
ancient	apart	consent	final
friendship	permit	shipwreck	sway

1. The king ruled an _____ city.

2. The cruel king did not _____ people to speak their ideas.

3. We all said goodbye on the _____ day of our trip.

4. The twins were never _____ from each other.

5. We tried to _____ her from going to the movie without us.

6. There was a terrible _____ during the big storm.

7. We will need the teacher's _____ to use the new computer.

8. Their _____ began when they were in third grade.

Understanding Fiction: Legend

A **legend** is a very old story that has been told through the ages. It is based on a real event and real people. Some facts may have changed as the story was told over and over. Look for these in a legend:

- a hero who does brave deeds
- real people and places from history

Write your answers to the questions about the legend.

1. A legend includes real places from history. Name two ancient places in the story.

   _____

   _____

2. Dionysius was a real person. He was the ruler of Syracuse and he was known for being cruel. Give the names of two more real people from the story. Tell about them.

   _____

   _____

3. Damon was one hero in the story. Describe his brave deed.

   _____

   _____

4. Pythias was another hero in the story. Describe his brave deed.

   _____

   _____

Name: _____

Literary Analysis: Plot

The **plot** is the order of events in a story. There is a beginning, middle, and ending. The characters move the plot along through their actions. Look for these things in the plot:

- A problem starts at the beginning.
- An uncertain feeling or a new character comes in the middle.
- The problem is settled at the end of the story.

Write your answers to the questions about the plot.

1. At the beginning of the story, what did Pythias do that started a problem?

   _____

2. Damon did all he could to help his friend. He even took his place in prison. Damon would be put to death if his friend did not return in time. What caused an uncertain feeling in the middle of the story?

   _____

   _____

3. How was the problem settled in the story's ending?

   _____

   _____

4. Write *beginning, middle,* or *ending* to tell when each event happened.

   a. The king's heart grew soft.   _____

   b. Damon was in prison.   _____

   c. Damon and Pythias were always together.   _____

   d. Pythias was in a shipwreck.   _____

Answer Questions

Use information from the legend to answer each question.

1. The subject of the story is _____.
   - Ⓐ ancient places
   - Ⓑ shipwrecks
   - Ⓒ famous kings
   - Ⓓ friendship

2. The story takes place _____.
   - Ⓐ in ancient times
   - Ⓑ in an unknown time
   - Ⓒ on a ship
   - Ⓓ today in Sicily

3. Dionysius was famous for being _____.
   - Ⓐ fair and wise
   - Ⓑ a great friend
   - Ⓒ trusting
   - Ⓓ cruel

4. What happened to Damon and Pythias at the end of the story?

   _____

   _____

5. What did the king learn from Damon and Pythias?

   _____

   _____

Name: _____

Literary Response

Write an opinion about the topic of friendship. Describe how people show friendship. Tell if you think Damon and Pythias were good friends to one another. Explain why you think so.

Friendship

_____

_____

_____

_____

_____

_____

_____

_____

_____

_____

_____

_____

_____

TE = Teacher's Edition
SB = Student Book

Answer Key

Unit 1

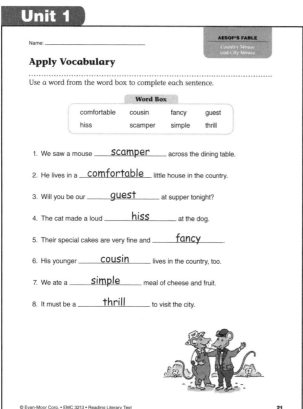

Name: _____

AESOP'S FABLE
Country Mouse
and City Mouse

Apply Vocabulary

Use a word from the word box to complete each sentence.

Word Box

comfortable	cousin	fancy	guest
hiss	scamper	simple	thrill

1. We saw a mouse ___scamper___ across the dining table.

2. He lives in a ___comfortable___ little house in the country.

3. Will you be our ___guest___ at supper tonight?

4. The cat made a loud ___hiss___ at the dog.

5. Their special cakes are very fine and ___fancy___.

6. His younger ___cousin___ lives in the country, too.

7. We ate a ___simple___ meal of cheese and fruit.

8. It must be a ___thrill___ to visit the city.

© Evan-Moor Corp. • EMC 3213 • Reading Literary Text   21

TE Page 21 / SB Page 10

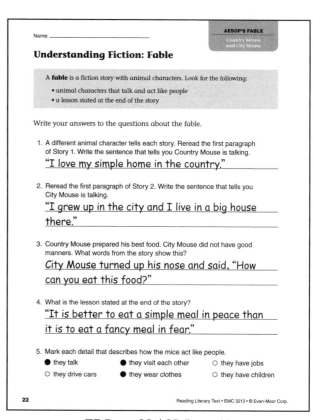

Name: _____

AESOP'S FABLE
Country Mouse
and City Mouse

Understanding Fiction: Fable

A **fable** is a fiction story with animal characters. Look for the following:
• animal characters that talk and act like people
• a lesson stated at the end of the story

Write your answers to the questions about the fable.

1. A different animal character tells each story. Reread the first paragraph of Story 1. Write the sentence that tells you Country Mouse is talking.
   "I love my simple home in the country."

2. Reread the first paragraph of Story 2. Write the sentence that tells you City Mouse is talking.
   "I grew up in the city and I live in a big house there."

3. Country Mouse prepared his best food. City Mouse did not have good manners. What words from the story show this?
   City Mouse turned up his nose and said, "How can you eat this food?"

4. What is the lesson stated at the end of the story?
   "It is better to eat a simple meal in peace than it is to eat a fancy meal in fear."

5. Mark each detail that describes how the mice act like people.
   ● they talk   ● they visit each other   ○ they have jobs
   ○ they drive cars   ● they wear clothes   ○ they have children

22   Reading Literary Text • EMC 3213 • © Evan-Moor Corp.

TE Page 22 / SB Page 11

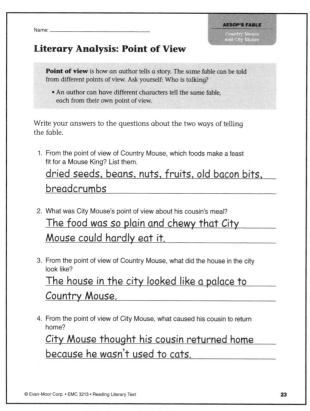

Name: _____

AESOP'S FABLE
Country Mouse
and City Mouse

Literary Analysis: Point of View

Point of view is how an author tells a story. The same fable can be told from different points of view. Ask yourself: Who is talking?
• An author can have different characters tell the same fable, each from their own point of view.

Write your answers to the questions about the two ways of telling the fable.

1. From the point of view of Country Mouse, which foods make a feast fit for a Mouse King? List them.
   dried seeds, beans, nuts, fruits, old bacon bits, breadcrumbs

2. What was City Mouse's point of view about his cousin's meal?
   The food was so plain and chewy that City Mouse could hardly eat it.

3. From the point of view of Country Mouse, what did the house in the city look like?
   The house in the city looked like a palace to Country Mouse.

4. From the point of view of City Mouse, what caused his cousin to return home?
   City Mouse thought his cousin returned home because he wasn't used to cats.

© Evan-Moor Corp. • EMC 3213 • Reading Literary Text   23

TE Page 23 / SB Page 12

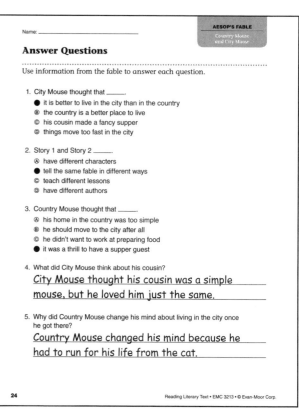

Name: _____

AESOP'S FABLE
Country Mouse
and City Mouse

Answer Questions

Use information from the fable to answer each question.

1. City Mouse thought that _____.
   ● it is better to live in the city than in the country
   ⓑ the country is a better place to live
   ⓒ his cousin made a fancy supper
   ⓓ things move too fast in the city

2. Story 1 and Story 2 _____.
   Ⓐ have different characters
   ● tell the same fable in different ways
   ⓒ teach different lessons
   ⓓ have different authors

3. Country Mouse thought that _____.
   Ⓐ his home in the country was too simple
   ⓑ he should move to the city after all
   ⓒ he didn't want to work at preparing food
   ● it was a thrill to have a supper guest

4. What did City Mouse think about his cousin?
   City Mouse thought his cousin was a simple mouse, but he loved him just the same.

5. Why did Country Mouse change his mind about living in the city once he got there?
   Country Mouse changed his mind because he had to run for his life from the cat.

24   Reading Literary Text • EMC 3213 • © Evan-Moor Corp.

TE Page 24 / SB Page 13

122   Reading Literary Text • EMC 3213 • © Evan-Moor Corp.

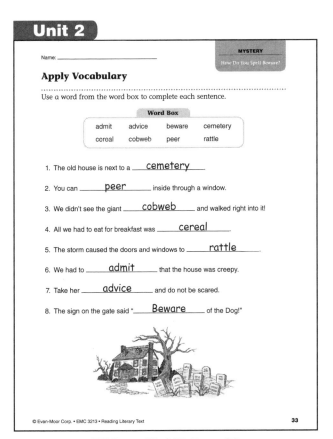

Apply Vocabulary

Use a word from the word box to complete each sentence.

Word Box

| admit | advice | beware | cemetery |
| cereal | cobweb | peer | rattle |

1. The old house is next to a ___cemetery___

2. You can ___peer___ inside through a window.

3. We didn't see the giant ___cobweb___ and walked right into it!

4. All we had to eat for breakfast was ___cereal___.

5. The storm caused the doors and windows to ___rattle___.

6. We had to ___admit___ that the house was creepy.

7. Take her ___advice___ and do not be scared.

8. The sign on the gate said "___Beware___ of the Dog!"

TE Page 33 / SB Page 20

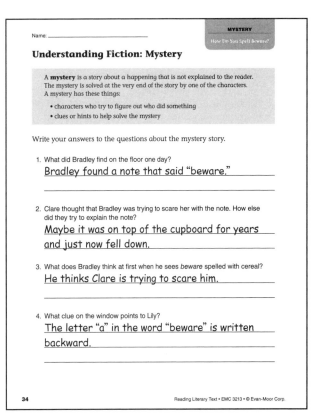

Understanding Fiction: Mystery

> A **mystery** is a story about a happening that is not explained to the reader. The mystery is solved at the very end of the story by one of the characters. A mystery has these things:
> • characters who try to figure out who did something
> • clues or hints to help solve the mystery

Write your answers to the questions about the mystery story.

1. What did Bradley find on the floor one day?
   Bradley found a note that said "beware."

2. Clare thought that Bradley was trying to scare her with the note. How else did they try to explain the note?
   Maybe it was on top of the cupboard for years and just now fell down.

3. What does Bradley think at first when he sees *beware* spelled with cereal?
   He thinks Clare is trying to scare him.

4. What clue on the window points to Lily?
   The letter "a" in the word "beware" is written backward.

TE Page 34 / SB Page 21

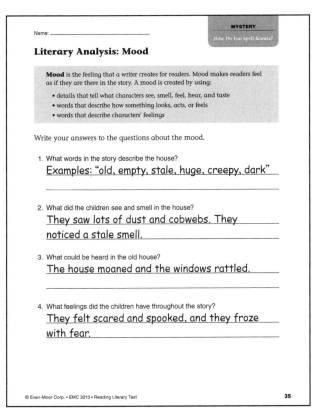

Literary Analysis: Mood

> **Mood** is the feeling that a writer creates for readers. Mood makes readers feel as if they are there in the story. A mood is created by using:
> • details that tell what characters see, smell, feel, hear, and taste
> • words that describe how something looks, acts, or feels
> • words that describe characters' feelings

Write your answers to the questions about the mood.

1. What words in the story describe the house?
   Examples: "old, empty, stale, huge, creepy, dark"

2. What did the children see and smell in the house?
   They saw lots of dust and cobwebs. They noticed a stale smell.

3. What could be heard in the old house?
   The house moaned and the windows rattled.

4. What feelings did the children have throughout the story?
   They felt scared and spooked, and they froze with fear.

TE Page 35 / SB Page 22

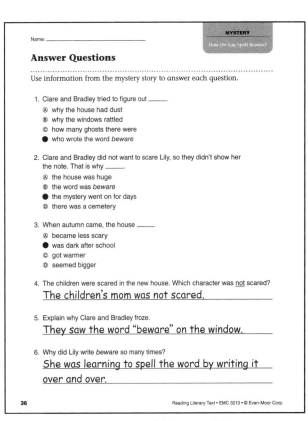

Answer Questions

Use information from the mystery story to answer each question.

1. Clare and Bradley tried to figure out _____.
   Ⓐ why the house had dust
   Ⓑ why the windows rattled
   Ⓒ how many ghosts there were
   ● who wrote the word *beware*

2. Clare and Bradley did not want to scare Lily, so they didn't show her the note. That is why _____.
   Ⓐ the house was huge
   Ⓑ the word was *beware*
   ● the mystery went on for days
   Ⓓ there was a cemetery

3. When autumn came, the house _____.
   Ⓐ became less scary
   ● was dark after school
   Ⓒ got warmer
   Ⓓ seemed bigger

4. The children were scared in the new house. Which character was <u>not</u> scared?
   The children's mom was not scared.

5. Explain why Clare and Bradley froze.
   They saw the word "beware" on the window.

6. Why did Lily write *beware* so many times?
   She was learning to spell the word by writing it over and over.

TE Page 36 / SB Page 23

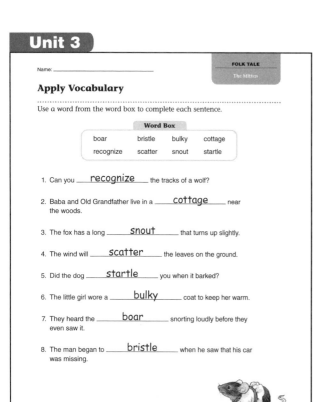

Name: _____

FOLK TALE
The Mitten

Apply Vocabulary

Use a word from the word box to complete each sentence.

Word Box			
boar	bristle	bulky	cottage
recognize	scatter	snout	startle

1. Can you ____recognize____ the tracks of a wolf?

2. Baba and Old Grandfather live in a ____cottage____ near the woods.

3. The fox has a long ____snout____ that turns up slightly.

4. The wind will ____scatter____ the leaves on the ground.

5. Did the dog ____startle____ you when it barked?

6. The little girl wore a ____bulky____ coat to keep her warm.

7. They heard the ____boar____ snorting loudly before they even saw it.

8. The man began to ____bristle____ when he saw that his car was missing.

© Evan-Moor Corp. • EMC 3213 • Reading Literary Text
45

TE Page 45 / SB Page 30

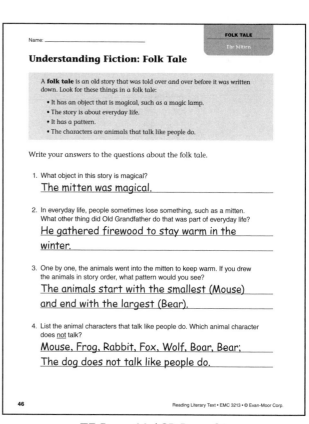

Name: _____

FOLK TALE
The Mitten

Understanding Fiction: Folk Tale

A **folk tale** is an old story that was told over and over before it was written down. Look for these things in a folk tale:

• It has an object that is magical, such as a magic lamp.
• The story is about everyday life.
• It has a pattern.
• The characters are animals that talk like people do.

Write your answers to the questions about the folk tale.

1. What object in this story is magical?
The mitten was magical.

2. In everyday life, people sometimes lose something, such as a mitten. What other thing did Old Grandfather do that was part of everyday life?
He gathered firewood to stay warm in the winter.

3. One by one, the animals went into the mitten to keep warm. If you drew the animals in story order, what pattern would you see?
The animals start with the smallest (Mouse) and end with the largest (Bear).

4. List the animal characters that talk like people do. Which animal character does not talk?
Mouse, Frog, Rabbit, Fox, Wolf, Boar, Bear;
The dog does not talk like people do.

46
Reading Literary Text • EMC 3213 • © Evan-Moor Corp.

TE Page 46 / SB Page 31

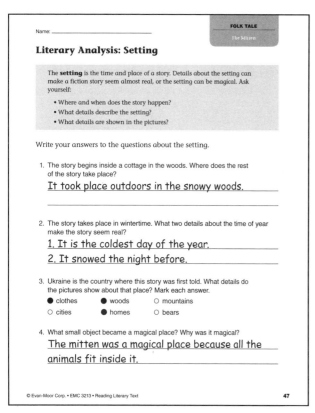

Name: _____

FOLK TALE
The Mitten

Literary Analysis: Setting

The **setting** is the time and place of a story. Details about the setting can make a fiction story seem almost real, or the setting can be magical. Ask yourself:

• Where and when does the story happen?
• What details describe the setting?
• What details are shown in the pictures?

Write your answers to the questions about the setting.

1. The story begins inside a cottage in the woods. Where does the rest of the story take place?
It took place outdoors in the snowy woods.

2. The story takes place in wintertime. What two details about the time of year make the story seem real?
1. It is the coldest day of the year.
2. It snowed the night before.

3. Ukraine is the country where this story was first told. What details do the pictures show about that place? Mark each answer.
● clothes   ● woods   ○ mountains
○ cities   ● homes   ○ bears

4. What small object became a magical place? Why was it magical?
The mitten was a magical place because all the animals fit inside it.

© Evan-Moor Corp. • EMC 3213 • Reading Literary Text
47

TE Page 47 / SB Page 32

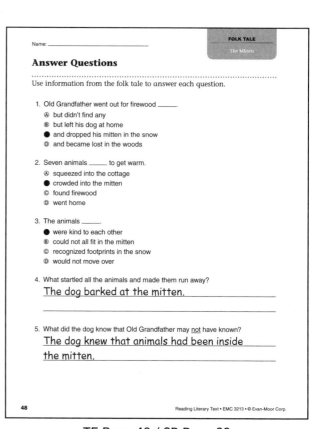

Name: _____

FOLK TALE
The Mitten

Answer Questions

Use information from the folk tale to answer each question.

1. Old Grandfather went out for firewood ____.
Ⓐ but didn't find any
Ⓑ but left his dog at home
● and dropped his mitten in the snow
Ⓓ and became lost in the woods

2. Seven animals ____ to get warm.
Ⓐ squeezed into the cottage
● crowded into the mitten
Ⓒ found firewood
Ⓓ went home

3. The animals ____.
● were kind to each other
Ⓑ could not all fit in the mitten
Ⓒ recognized footprints in the snow
Ⓓ would not move over

4. What startled all the animals and made them run away?
The dog barked at the mitten.

5. What did the dog know that Old Grandfather may not have known?
The dog knew that animals had been inside the mitten.

48
Reading Literary Text • EMC 3213 • © Evan-Moor Corp.

TE Page 48 / SB Page 33

Reading Literary Text • EMC 3213 • © Evan-Moor Corp.

Page 57 (left top)

Name: _____

CLASSIC LITERATURE
Rebecca's School Day

Apply Vocabulary

Use a word from the word box to complete each sentence.

Word Box

blackboard	conduct	exact	platform
punish	scholar	subject	uncomfortable

1. Some students sat on **uncomfortable** wooden benches.

2. The teacher asked a boy to erase the lesson on the **blackboard**

3. It is a rule of good **conduct** to raise your hand before speaking.

4. What is the **subject** of the poem you are learning?

5. The young **scholar** answered the question correctly.

6. The teacher would **punish** those who did not work quietly.

7. The teacher stood on a **platform** so everyone could see her.

8. Rebecca counted the **exact** number of books needed for the class.

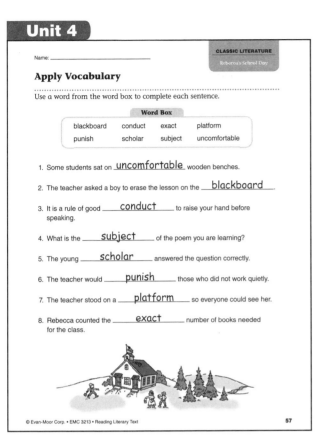

© Evan-Moor Corp. • EMC 3213 • Reading Literary Text   57

TE Page 57 / SB Page 40

Page 58 (right top)

Name: _____

CLASSIC LITERATURE
Rebecca's School Day

Understanding Fiction: Classic Literature

A **classic literature** story is thought to be one of the best ever written. Some words in a classic story may sound old-fashioned to us today. Some classic stories tell us about life in times long ago.

Write your answers to the questions about the classic literature story.

1. Some words in a classic story are not used as often today. What word did the author use instead of "students"?

   "scholars"

2. An author can show us what life was like long ago. For example, how did the scholars in Rebecca's school get a drink of water?

   They asked the teacher first. Then they could walk to the tin water pail and drink from the long-handled dipper.

3. Which of these tell you that Rebecca's school was different from schools today?

   - ● there was a pot-bellied stove
   - ● there was one door for boys, one door for girls
   - ○ there were swings and slides
   - ○ there were blackboards
   - ● there was a water pail and dipper
   - ○ there were wooden desks and benches
   - ● there was only one teacher
   - ○ there were windows

4. Rebecca walked a mile to school. Which of these did she like to do along the way?

   - ● startle the frogs
   - ● wave away the cows
   - ○ fish for mackerel
   - ● say her poem
   - ● take a shortcut
   - ○ sing "The Old Oaken Bucket"
   - ● jump from stone to stone
   - ● swing her dinner pail

58   Reading Literary Text • EMC 3213 • © Evan-Moor Corp.

TE Page 58 / SB Page 41

Page 59 (left bottom)

Name: _____

CLASSIC LITERATURE
Rebecca's School Day

Literary Analysis: Character

When you think about a **character**, it helps you better understand that character. You can get to know the character by thinking about the following:

- what a character does
- what a character thinks
- what a character says
- how the author describes a character

Write your answers to the questions about the characters.

1. An author can show us how a character feels by the person's actions. List three things Miss Dearborn did that show how she felt. **Answers will vary—Example:**

   1. She raised her eyebrows.
   2. She sent Rebecca to stand by the pail.
   3. She gave Alice a warning look.

2. Write one thing Rebecca thought that tells how she was feeling. **Answers will vary—Example:**

   She thought that she couldn't bear to be punished at the same time as Sam.

3. List three things the author wrote about Sam Simpson that helped you know more about him.

   1. He followed what Rebecca did and asked to get a drink each time she got one.
   2. He had a hard time making up his mind about anything.
   3. He changed his mind a lot, so they called him "Seesaw."

© Evan-Moor Corp. • EMC 3213 • Reading Literary Text   59

TE Page 59 / SB Page 42

Page 60 (right bottom)

Name: _____

CLASSIC LITERATURE
Rebecca's School Day

Answer Questions

Use information from the story to answer each question.

1. Rebecca went to _____.
   - Ⓐ a school in another town
   - ● a one-room schoolhouse
   - Ⓒ an old oaken school
   - Ⓓ a large school with many classrooms

2. In Rebecca's school, you would find _____.
   - Ⓐ computers
   - Ⓑ a drinking fountain
   - Ⓒ whiteboards and markers
   - ● a pail of water

3. Miss Dearborn raised her eyebrows because _____.
   - Ⓐ she was being silly
   - Ⓑ Rebecca wanted to sit near the window
   - ● Rebecca had asked for too many drinks
   - Ⓓ she didn't like salt mackerel

4. Why did Miss Dearborn punish Rebecca?

   She wanted to end the silly habit of getting drinks.

5. Why did the scholars want to sit in the back of the class?

   They wanted to be closer to the windows and farther from the teacher.

60   Reading Literary Text • EMC 3213 • © Evan-Moor Corp.

TE Page 60 / SB Page 43

© Evan-Moor Corp. • EMC 3213 • Reading Literary Text   **125**

Page 1 (TE Page 69 / SB Page 50)

Name: _____

FAIRY TALE
Never Kick a Slipper
at the Moon

Apply Vocabulary

Use a word from the word box to complete each sentence.

Word Box

closet	fasten	lag	pigeon-toed
straight	stumble	tumble	two-step

1. Everyone made a circle and danced the ___two-step___.

2. The slippers danced out of the ___closet___.

3. Her slipper went ___straight___ up to the moon.

4. The tired little dancer will ___tumble___ into bed.

5. Can a dancing slipper ___fasten___ itself to the moon?

6. The slower dancers always ___lag___ behind us.

7. The tired dancers will ___stumble___ out of the room.

8. Turn your toes in and walk ___pigeon-toed___.

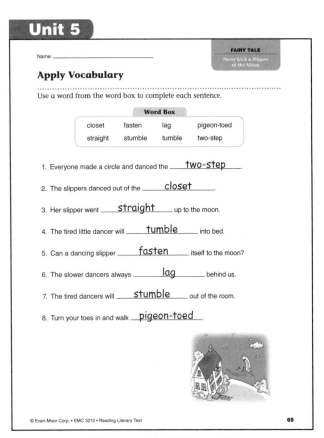

© Evan-Moor Corp. • EMC 3213 • Reading Literary Text   69

TE Page 69 / SB Page 50

Page 2 (TE Page 70 / SB Page 51)

Name: _____

FAIRY TALE
Never Kick a Slipper
at the Moon

Understanding Fiction: Fairy Tale

A **fairy tale** is a make-believe story that is told as if it were true. A fairy tale may have magic in it. Many fairy tales have happy endings.

Write your answers to the questions about the fairy tale.

1. Who tells the story of the Dancing Slipper Moon?
   Mr. Wishes

2. Like most fathers do, Mr. Wishes tells his daughter what to do and what not to do. What does he tell her?
   He tells her to never kick a slipper at a Dancing Slipper Moon.

3. What magical thing happened one night while people were asleep?
   The shoes and the slippers and the boots walked out of the bedrooms and closets.

4. What magical thing happened at the end of the story?
   The girl's slipper flew up to the moon and was never seen again.

5. Did this fairy tale have a happy ending? Explain why or why not.
   Answers will vary.

70   Reading Literary Text • EMC 3213 • © Evan-Moor Corp.

TE Page 70 / SB Page 51

Page 3 (TE Page 71 / SB Page 52)

Name: _____

FAIRY TALE
Never Kick a Slipper
at the Moon

Literary Analysis: Setting

The **setting** is where a story takes place. The setting can make the story seem real or make-believe. In a make-believe place, magical things may happen. Ask yourself:
- Does the story take place in a real place?
- Does the story take place in a make-believe place with a made-up name?

Write your answers to the questions about the setting.

1. Where do Mr. Wishes and his daughter live?
   They live in Rootabaga Country.

2. The girl who kicked her slipper to the moon lives in the Village of Cream Puffs. What things make this village seem make-believe? Explain your answer.
   The Village of Cream Puffs seems make-believe because shoes can walk by themselves and there is a moon that keeps slippers.

3. What things make the Village of Cream Puffs seem real? Explain your answer.
   The girl lives in a house; she went to a dance and was tired; she wears dancing slippers; she can see the moon in the sky.

4. Do the names of places in the story seem real or make-believe? Explain why.
   Answers will vary.

© Evan-Moor Corp. • EMC 3213 • Reading Literary Text   71

TE Page 71 / SB Page 52

Page 4 (TE Page 72 / SB Page 53)

Name: _____

FAIRY TALE
Never Kick a Slipper
at the Moon

Answer Questions

Use information from the fairy tale to answer each question.

1. The Dancing Slipper Moon is _____.
   Ⓐ a slipper
   Ⓑ a real place
   ● make-believe
   Ⓓ in the deep blue sea

2. Mr. Wishes tells his daughter _____.
   ● a bedtime story
   Ⓑ how to dance a two-step
   Ⓒ why the moon changes
   Ⓓ to put her shoes in the closet

3. All the shoes, slippers, and boots _____.
   Ⓐ wished to go to the moon
   Ⓑ were never seen again
   Ⓒ were sleeping
   ● walked out of the closets

4. Why did the girl kick her dancing slipper at the moon?
   She was happy when she saw the moon. She was singing.

5. Mr. Wishes says to never kick a slipper at the moon. Why?
   Because the slipper will go straight up to the moon. It will fasten itself to the moon and never come back.

72   Reading Literary Text • EMC 3213 • © Evan-Moor Corp.

TE Page 72 / SB Page 53

TE Page 81 / SB Page 60

Name: _____

TALL TALE
Davy Crockett
Escapes a Tornado

Apply Vocabulary

Use a word from the word box to complete each sentence.

Word Box

bolt	captain	escape	mighty
Niagara Falls	rumble	squirm	wrestle

1. Davy Crockett was strong enough to ___wrestle___ a bear.

2. We heard the ___rumble___ of thunder in the distance.

3. There was a ___mighty___ storm that day.

4. Boats rocked when the water began to ___squirm___.

5. The ship's ___captain___ said that a storm was coming.

6. A ___bolt___ of lightning flashed across the sky.

7. The noise was as loud as ___Niagara Falls___.

8. Davy and Ben thought it was time to ___escape___.

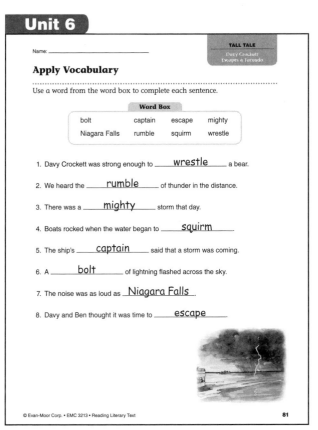

© Evan-Moor Corp. • EMC 3213 • Reading Literary Text · 81

TE Page 82 / SB Page 61

Name: _____

TALL TALE
Davy Crockett
Escapes a Tornado

Understanding Fiction: Tall Tale

An American **tall tale** is an old story about a larger-than-life character that is a hero. A hero is sometimes based on a real person. The story is told as if it were true. However, a tall tale stretches the truth.

Write your answers to the questions about the tall tale.

1. Davy Crockett was a real person. He was alive when America was a young country. Who tells this story?
   Davy Crockett tells this story.

2. Davy Crockett is a larger-than-life character. List two things he could do that show how strong and brave he was. Examples:
   He could wrestle a bear.
   He could tame an alligator.

3. This story stretches the truth. How did Davy Crockett and Ben Hardin escape the tornado?
   They jumped onto a lightning bolt and left the tornado behind them.

4. Mark all the things that make this story a tall tale.
   ● A person cannot ride a lightning bolt.
   ● Davy Crockett was a real person.
   ○ Davy Crockett and Ben Hardin were friends.
   ● Davy greased a lightning bolt with rattlesnake oil.

82 · Reading Literary Text • EMC 3213 • © Evan-Moor Corp.

TE Page 83 / SB Page 62

Name: _____

TALL TALE
Davy Crockett
Escapes a Tornado

Literary Analysis: Character

When you think about what a **character** says and does, it helps you to better understand that character. You can also think about the following:
• what the character thinks
• how the character changes
• how the author describes the character
• the character's relationships with others

Write your answers to the questions about the main character.

1. Do you think Davy Crockett was a quiet person or a loud person? Give an example from the story. Examples:
   He was a loud person. His voice was about as loud as low thunder.

2. How do you know that Davy Crockett didn't like the way folks in Washington ran the country? Write his words from the story.
   "It's for sure I could show those folks how to run the country."

3. What action words are used to describe what Davy Crockett did?
   "escaped," "rumbled," "wrestle," "tame," "boomed," "grabbed," "sprang," "rode," "grease," "streaked"

4. Davy said that he could wrestle a bear and tame an alligator. What does that tell you about Davy?
   He was strong and brave.

© Evan-Moor Corp. • EMC 3213 • Reading Literary Text · 83

TE Page 84 / SB Page 63

Name: _____

TALL TALE
Davy Crockett
Escapes a Tornado

Answer Questions

Use information from the tall tale to answer each question.

1. The story "Davy Crockett Escapes a Tornado" is told by _____.
   Ⓐ a person who saw it happen
   Ⓑ Ben Hardin
   Ⓒ a steamboat captain
   ● Davy himself

2. The story takes place _____.
   Ⓐ in a make-believe place
   Ⓑ today at Natchez
   ● long ago on the Mississippi River
   Ⓓ at Niagara Falls

3. Davy Crockett _____.
   ● said he rode a lightning bolt
   Ⓑ was a steamboat captain
   Ⓒ didn't like to talk about himself
   Ⓓ was afraid of lightning

4. How did Davy describe the sound of the tornado?
   He said it was "a roar that would have made old Niagara sound like a kitten."

5. The saying "as fast as greased lightning" describes something that moves very fast. How was that idea used in this story?
   Davy greased a lightning bolt with rattlesnake oil to escape the tornado.

84 · Reading Literary Text • EMC 3213 • © Evan-Moor Corp.

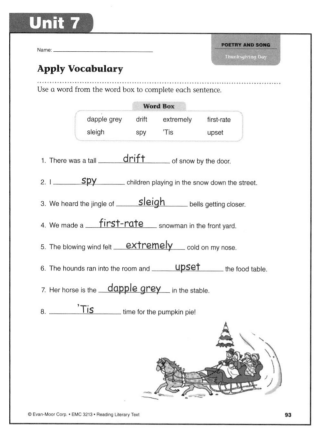

TE Page 93 / SB Page 70

Apply Vocabulary

Use a word from the word box to complete each sentence.

Word Box

dapple grey	drift	extremely	first-rate
sleigh	spy	'Tis	upset

1. There was a tall ___drift___ of snow by the door.

2. I ___spy___ children playing in the snow down the street.

3. We heard the jingle of ___sleigh___ bells getting closer.

4. We made a ___first-rate___ snowman in the front yard.

5. The blowing wind felt ___extremely___ cold on my nose.

6. The hounds ran into the room and ___upset___ the food table.

7. Her horse is the ___dapple grey___ in the stable.

8. ___'Tis___ time for the pumpkin pie!

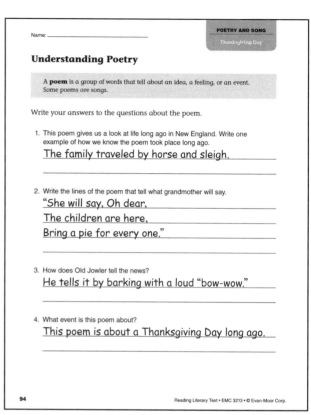

TE Page 94 / SB Page 71

Understanding Poetry

A **poem** is a group of words that tell about an idea, a feeling, or an event. Some poems are songs.

Write your answers to the questions about the poem.

1. This poem gives us a look at life long ago in New England. Write one example of how we know the poem took place long ago.
   The family traveled by horse and sleigh.

2. Write the lines of the poem that tell what grandmother will say.
   "She will say, Oh dear,
   The children are here,
   Bring a pie for every one."

3. How does Old Jowler tell the news?
   He tells it by barking with a loud "bow-wow."

4. What event is this poem about?
   This poem is about a Thanksgiving Day long ago.

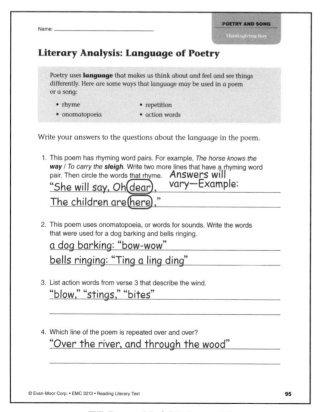

TE Page 95 / SB Page 72

Literary Analysis: Language of Poetry

Poetry uses **language** that makes us think about and feel and see things differently. Here are some ways that language may be used in a poem or a song:

- rhyme
- onomatopoeia
- repetition
- action words

Write your answers to the questions about the language in the poem.

1. This poem has rhyming word pairs. For example, *The horse knows the way / To carry the sleigh*. Write two more lines that have a rhyming word pair. Then circle the words that rhyme. Answers will vary—Example:
   "She will say, Oh (dear),
   The children are (here),"

2. This poem uses onomatopoeia, or words for sounds. Write the words that were used for a dog barking and bells ringing.
   a dog barking: "bow-wow"
   bells ringing: "Ting a ling ding"

3. List action words from verse 3 that describe the wind.
   "blow," "stings," "bites"

4. Which line of the poem is repeated over and over?
   "Over the river, and through the wood"

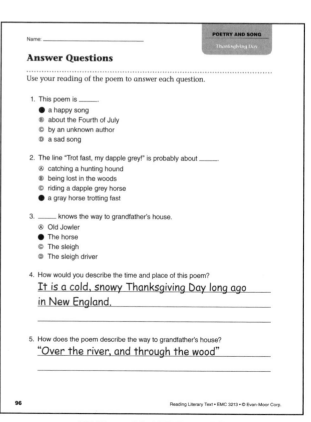

TE Page 96 / SB Page 73

Answer Questions

Use your reading of the poem to answer each question.

1. This poem is _____.
   ● a happy song
   ⑧ about the Fourth of July
   ⑨ by an unknown author
   ⑩ a sad song

2. The line "Trot fast, my dapple grey!" is probably about _____.
   Ⓐ catching a hunting hound
   ⑧ being lost in the woods
   ⑨ riding a dapple grey horse
   ● a gray horse trotting fast

3. _____ knows the way to grandfather's house.
   Ⓐ Old Jowler
   ● The horse
   ⑨ The sleigh
   ⑩ The sleigh driver

4. How would you describe the time and place of this poem?
   It is a cold, snowy Thanksgiving Day long ago in New England.

5. How does the poem describe the way to grandfather's house?
   "Over the river, and through the wood"

TE Page 105 (SB Page 80)

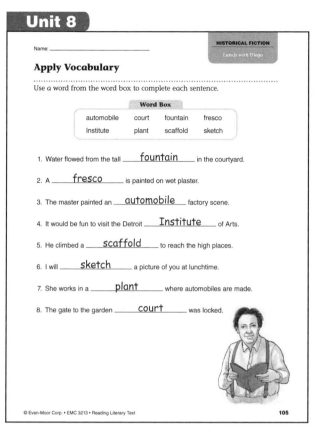

HISTORICAL FICTION
Lunch with Diego

Name: _____

Apply Vocabulary

Use a word from the word box to complete each sentence.

Word Box

automobile	court	fountain	fresco
Institute	plant	scaffold	sketch

1. Water flowed from the tall _____fountain_____ in the courtyard.

2. A _____fresco_____ is painted on wet plaster.

3. The master painted an _____automobile_____ factory scene.

4. It would be fun to visit the Detroit _____Institute_____ of Arts.

5. He climbed a _____scaffold_____ to reach the high places.

6. I will _____sketch_____ a picture of you at lunchtime.

7. She works in a _____plant_____ where automobiles are made.

8. The gate to the garden _____court_____ was locked.

© Evan-Moor Corp. • EMC 3213 • Reading Literary Text   105

TE Page 105 / SB Page 80

TE Page 106 (SB Page 81)

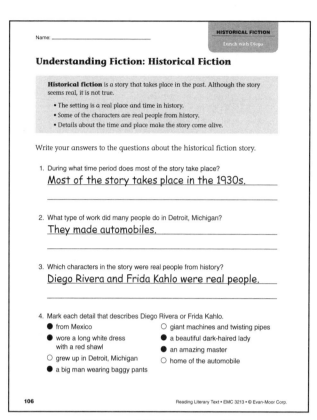

HISTORICAL FICTION
Lunch with Diego

Name: _____

Understanding Fiction: Historical Fiction

Historical fiction is a story that takes place in the past. Although the story seems real, it is not true.
- The setting is a real place and time in history.
- Some of the characters are real people from history.
- Details about the time and place make the story come alive.

Write your answers to the questions about the historical fiction story.

1. During what time period does most of the story take place?
   Most of the story takes place in the 1930s.

2. What type of work did many people do in Detroit, Michigan?
   They made automobiles.

3. Which characters in the story were real people from history?
   Diego Rivera and Frida Kahlo were real people.

4. Mark each detail that describes Diego Rivera or Frida Kahlo.
   - ● from Mexico
   - ● wore a long white dress with a red shawl
   - ○ grew up in Detroit, Michigan
   - ● a big man wearing baggy pants
   - ○ giant machines and twisting pipes
   - ● a beautiful dark-haired lady
   - ● an amazing master
   - ○ home of the automobile

106   Reading Literary Text • EMC 3213 • © Evan-Moor Corp.

TE Page 106 / SB Page 81

TE Page 107 (SB Page 82)

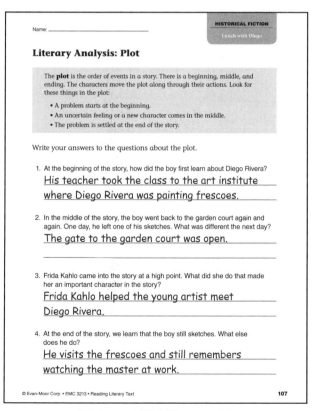

HISTORICAL FICTION
Lunch with Diego

Name: _____

Literary Analysis: Plot

The **plot** is the order of events in a story. There is a beginning, middle, and ending. The characters move the plot along through their actions. Look for these things in the plot:
- A problem starts at the beginning.
- An uncertain feeling or a new character comes in the middle.
- The problem is settled at the end of the story.

Write your answers to the questions about the plot.

1. At the beginning of the story, how did the boy first learn about Diego Rivera?
   His teacher took the class to the art institute where Diego Rivera was painting frescoes.

2. In the middle of the story, the boy went back to the garden court again and again. One day, he left one of his sketches. What was different the next day?
   The gate to the garden court was open.

3. Frida Kahlo came into the story at a high point. What did she do that made her an important character in the story?
   Frida Kahlo helped the young artist meet Diego Rivera.

4. At the end of the story, we learn that the boy still sketches. What else does he do?
   He visits the frescoes and still remembers watching the master at work.

© Evan-Moor Corp. • EMC 3213 • Reading Literary Text   107

TE Page 107 / SB Page 82

TE Page 108 (SB Page 83)

HISTORICAL FICTION
Lunch with Diego

Name: _____

Answer Questions

Use information from the historical fiction story to answer each question.

1. In this story, Diego Rivera painted frescoes _____.
   - Ⓐ with the help of children
   - ● of workers and machines
   - Ⓒ in a school in Detroit
   - Ⓓ of his wife, Frida Kahlo

2. Every day, the boy went _____.
   - Ⓐ to art class
   - ● to watch Diego Rivera paint
   - Ⓒ with his teacher to the garden court
   - Ⓓ home for lunch

3. One day, the boy was able to _____.
   - Ⓐ paint a fresco
   - Ⓑ play in the fountain
   - ● meet the master artist
   - Ⓓ visit an automobile plant

4. What did the boy leave behind that led to his meeting Diego Rivera?
   He left behind his sketch of the beautiful dark-haired lady.

5. Explain why you think the boy did not speak to Diego or Frida.
   I think the boy was shy because Diego was a great painter, and he was also shocked that they were looking at his sketches.

108   Reading Literary Text • EMC 3213 • © Evan-Moor Corp.

TE Page 108 / SB Page 83

Apply Vocabulary

Name: _____

Use a word from the word box to complete each sentence.

Word Box

| ancient | apart | consent | final |
| friendship | permit | shipwreck | sway |

1. The king ruled an _____ancient_____ city.

2. The cruel king did not _____permit_____ people to speak their ideas.

3. We all said goodbye on the _____final_____ day of our trip.

4. The twins were never _____apart_____ from each other.

5. We tried to _____sway_____ her from going to the movie without us.

6. There was a terrible _____shipwreck_____ during the big storm.

7. We will need the teacher's _____consent_____ to use the new computer.

8. Their _____friendship_____ began when they were in third grade.

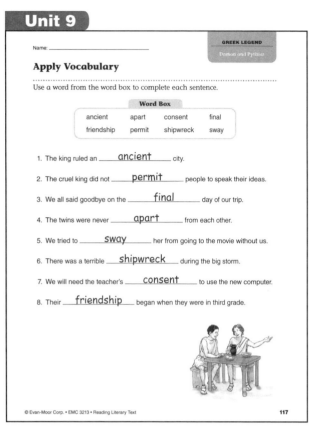

TE Page 117 / SB Page 90

Name: _____

Understanding Fiction: Legend

A **legend** is a very old story that has been told through the ages. It is based on a real event and real people. Some facts may have changed as the story was told over and over. Look for these in a legend:

• a hero who does brave deeds
• real people and places from history

Write your answers to the questions about the legend.

1. A legend includes real places from history. Name two ancient places in the story.
the city of Syracuse and the island of Sicily

2. Dionysius was a real person. He was the ruler of Syracuse and he was known for being cruel. Give the names of two more real people from the story. Tell about them.
Damon and Pythias were two young men from Syracuse who were best friends.

3. Damon was one hero in the story. Describe his brave deed.
He took his friend's place in prison and was ready to die for him.

4. Pythias was another hero in the story. Describe his brave deed.
He returned to save his friend and face death.

TE Page 118 / SB Page 91

Name: _____

Literary Analysis: Plot

The **plot** is the order of events in a story. There is a beginning, middle, and ending. The characters move the plot along through their actions. Look for these things in the plot:

• A problem starts at the beginning.
• An uncertain feeling or a new character comes in the middle.
• The problem is settled at the end of the story.

Write your answers to the questions about the plot.

1. At the beginning of the story, what did Pythias do that started a problem?
Pythias spoke out against the king.

2. Damon did all he could to help his friend. He even took his place in prison. Damon would be put to death if his friend did not return in time. What caused an uncertain feeling in the middle of the story?
The final day was getting closer, and Pythias had not yet returned.

3. How was the problem settled in the story's ending?
Pythias returned in time to save Damon. The king changed his mind and set them both free.

4. Write *beginning, middle,* or *ending* to tell when each event happened.

   a. The king's heart grew soft. _____ending_____

   b. Damon was in prison. _____middle_____

   c. Damon and Pythias were always together. _____beginning_____

   d. Pythias was in a shipwreck. _____middle_____

TE Page 119 / SB Page 92

Name: _____

Answer Questions

Use information from the legend to answer each question.

1. The subject of the story is _____.
   Ⓐ ancient places
   Ⓑ shipwrecks
   Ⓒ famous kings
   ● friendship

2. The story takes place _____.
   ● in ancient times
   Ⓑ in an unknown time
   Ⓒ on a ship
   Ⓓ today in Sicily

3. Dionysius was famous for being _____.
   Ⓐ fair and wise
   Ⓑ a great friend
   Ⓒ trusting
   ● cruel

4. What happened to Damon and Pythias at the end of the story?
They both were set free.

5. What did the king learn from Damon and Pythias?
The king learned what true friendship is.

TE Page 120 / SB Page 93

Common Core Lessons

Reading Informational Text

Grade 3

SAMPLER

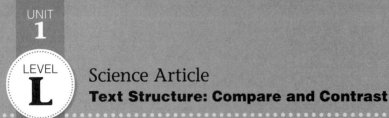

LEVEL
L

Science Article
Text Structure: Compare and Contrast

Big, Wild Cats!

Lesson Objective	Students will explain how a tiger moves, eats, and lives in the forests and jungles of Asia.
Content Knowledge	Animals depend on the land, water, and air to live and grow.

Lesson Preparation

Reproduce and distribute one copy of the article, dictionary page, and activity pages to each student.

Learn		PAGE
1	Read Aloud the Article	14–15
2	Introduce the Vocabulary	16
3	Students Read the Article	

Analyze		
4	Identify Information	17
5	Answer Questions	18
6	Apply Vocabulary	19
7	Examine Text Structure	20

Write		
8	Write About It: *A Tiger's Life*	21

SCIENCE
Big, Wild Cats!

Name: _____

Big, Wild Cats!

The roar of a lion or a tiger can make a person shake with fear. Lions and tigers are close relatives, but they have differences, too.

Where Lions and Tigers Live

These big cats both live in the wild. However, they live in different parts of the world. Lions live in the grasslands of Africa. Their sandy-colored fur blends in with the tall yellow grasses. Tigers live in forests and jungles in Asia. Their orange fur has dark stripes that help them hide among trees. No two tigers have the same pattern of stripes.

The weather is hot where lions and tigers live. Lions like to stay dry. They go into water only if they have to. However, tigers are good swimmers. They may swim across rivers to hunt. They also go into water to cool off.

How Big Cats Live

Both kinds of big cats live and hunt in an area that covers many miles. This area is their *territory*. Lions live in family groups called *prides*. A pride has males, females, and their cubs. Each pride has its own territory. Lions roar to guard their territory. An adult lion's roar can be heard up to five miles away.

Unlike lions, tigers do not live in groups. A mother tiger raises her cubs without their father. The cubs stay with their mother for only two years. Then they live alone in their own territory.

Lions live in family groups called prides.

Reading Informational Text • EMC 3203 • © Evan-Moor Corp.

14

...and tigers are in danger. Many lions die from sicknesses caused by hot weather and not enough water. Also, lions are losing their territories because people are using the land to grow food. Long ago, lions were found in Africa, Asia, and Europe. Today, they live only in Africa and in one forest in India.

Some people hunt tigers for their skin and other parts. Tigers are losing their territories as forests are cut down. Tigers used to live in many parts of Asia. Today, they live only in small areas. Many people are working to save lions and tigers.

Unlike lions, tigers hunt alone. This tiger is creeping toward its prey.

© Evan-Moor Corp. • EMC 3203 • Reading Informational Text

15

CCSS: RIT 3.1, 3.2, 3.3, 3.4, 3.5, 3.7, 3.8   W 3.2

1 Read Aloud the Article

Read aloud *Big, Wild Cats!* Have students follow along silently as you read.

2 Introduce the Vocabulary

Content Vocabulary
Read aloud the Content Vocabulary words and definitions. Point out that *grasslands* is a compound word that contains the words *grass* and *lands*. The two words give clues about the meaning of the word. Explain that *sandy-colored* is another compound word used in the article. It is a describing word that has a hyphen connecting its two word parts. Discuss definitions and usage as needed.

Academic Vocabulary
Next, read aloud the Academic Vocabulary words and definitions. Discuss definitions and usage as needed. Then read these context sentences from the article, emphasizing the Academic Vocabulary words:

*Lions and tigers are close **relatives**, but they have differences, too.*

*A pride has **males**, **females**, and their cubs.*

*An **adult** lion's roar can be heard up to five miles away.*

3 Students Read the Article

Have students read the article independently, with a partner, or in small groups. After students read, guide a discussion about the article. Direct students' attention to graphic elements or visual aids.

4 Identify Information

Explain that students will locate important information in the article. After students complete the activity, allow time for a question-and-answer session.

5 Answer Questions

Encourage students to use the article to answer the questions and/or check their answers.

6 Apply Vocabulary

Have students reread the article before they complete the vocabulary activity. Optional: Have students mark each vocabulary word as they read.

7 Examine Text Structure

Read aloud the Compare and Contrast description and Signal Words. Then have students read the article again, underlining signal words in red. Then guide students in completing the activity.

8 Write About It:
A Tiger's Life

Have students complete the writing activity independently or in small groups.

Name: _____

Big, Wild Cats!

The roar of a lion or a tiger can make a person shake with fear. Lions and tigers are close relatives, but they have differences, too.

Where Lions and Tigers Live

These big cats both live in the wild. However, they live in different parts of the world. Lions live in the grasslands of Africa. Their sandy-colored fur blends in with the tall yellow grasses. Tigers live in forests and jungles in Asia. Their orange fur has dark stripes that help them hide among trees. No two tigers have the same pattern of stripes.

The weather is hot where lions and tigers live. Lions like to stay dry. They go into water only if they have to. However, tigers are good swimmers. They may swim across rivers to hunt. They also go into water to cool off.

How Big Cats Live

Both kinds of big cats live and hunt in an area that covers many miles. This area is their *territory*. Lions live in family groups called *prides*. A pride has males, females, and their cubs. Each pride has its own territory. Lions roar to guard their territory. An adult lion's roar can be heard up to five miles away.

Lions live in family groups called prides.

Unlike lions, tigers do not live in groups. A mother tiger raises her cubs without their father. The cubs stay with their mother for only two years. Then they live alone in their own territory.

How Lions and Tigers Catch Their Food

Lions and tigers are meat eaters. Both kinds of cats are strong hunters that have sharp teeth and claws. Lions and tigers both creep up on their prey and attack by surprise. Female lions do most of the hunting. They may work as a team to hunt animals that are faster than they are. Unlike lions, tigers hunt alone.

Dangers to Big Cats

Both lions and tigers are in danger. Many lions die from sicknesses caused by hot weather and not enough water. Also, lions are losing their territories because people are using the land to grow food. Long ago, lions were found in Africa, Asia, and Europe. Today, they live only in Africa and in one forest in India.

Unlike lions, tigers hunt alone. This tiger is creeping toward its prey.

Some people hunt tigers for their skin and other parts. Tigers are losing their territories as forests are cut down. Tigers used to live in many parts of Asia. Today, they live only in small areas. Many people are working to save lions and tigers.

Name: _____

Dictionary

Content Vocabulary

attack
to try to hurt or kill

forests
areas of land where many trees grow

grasslands
areas of land that are covered with grasses but not trees or bushes

jungles
areas of land that are thickly covered with bushes, trees, and vines

prey
animals that are hunted and eaten by other animals

Academic Vocabulary

relatives
members of the same family or animal group

males
animals that can be the father of young

females
animals that can be the mother of young

adult
a full-grown animal

Write a sentence that includes a vocabulary word.

_____

_____

Identify Information

You can understand a text better if you read it more than once. Look for the following information as you read the article again. Put a check mark in the box after you complete each task.

		I did it!
🖊	Highlight any words that describe where lions live.	☐
☐	Draw a box around any words that describe where tigers live.	☐
◯	Circle four words that describe the fur of lions and tigers.	☐
—	Draw a line under the sentence that explains how tigers cool off.	☐
[ ]	Put brackets around the sentences that explain what a territory is.	☐
★	Draw a star next to the paragraph about how lions and tigers hunt.	☐
✖	Put an X next to each paragraph that explains why people are working to save lions and tigers.	☐
▲	Draw a triangle next to any information that surprised or interested you.	☐
?	Put a question mark beside any words or sentences you don't understand.	☐

Answer Questions

Use information from the article to answer each question.

1. Lions live in Africa's grasslands, but tigers live in _____.
   - Ⓐ Africa's forests
   - Ⓑ Asia's grasslands
   - Ⓒ Asia's jungles
   - Ⓓ Africa and Asia

2. Both lions and tigers have _____.
   - Ⓐ prides
   - Ⓑ their own territories
   - Ⓒ dark stripes
   - Ⓓ sandy-colored fur

3. When they hunt, both kinds of big cats _____.
   - Ⓐ attack by surprise
   - Ⓑ roar loudly
   - Ⓒ work as a team
   - Ⓓ work alone

4. How does a lion's fur help it live in the wild?

   _____

   _____

5. How does a tiger's fur help it live in the wild?

   _____

   _____

Name: _____

Apply Vocabulary

Use a word from the word box to complete each sentence.

Word Box		
females	grasslands	prey
jungles	relatives	males
attack	forests	adult

1. Lions blend in with Africa's _____ because of the color of their fur.

2. Among lions, _____ do most of the hunting.

3. Tigers and lions are both cats, which makes them _____.

4. Animals that live in forests and _____ are food for tigers.

5. A team of female lions may work together to hunt _____.

6. Among tigers, the _____ do not help raise their own cubs.

7. An _____ lion's roar can be heard miles away.

8. Tigers can be found in _____ and jungles throughout Asia.

9. Lions and tigers use sharp teeth and claws to _____ their prey.

Name: _____

Compare and Contrast

....

A text that has a **compare-and-contrast** structure is about two main ideas. It tells how the two ideas are alike (compares). It also tells how the two ideas are different (contrasts).

Authors use these signal words to create a **compare-and-contrast** structure:

Signal Words

both	today	but
long ago	however	unlike

1. The first paragraph tells us that the article will compare and contrast what two things?

   _____

2. Write the sentence that tells how tigers are different from lions in the way they live.

   _____

   _____

3. Are lions and tigers alike or different in what they eat? Write the sentence from the article that tells you how they are similar or different.

   _____

   _____

Write About It

....

Explain how a tiger moves, eats, and lives in the forests and jungles
of Asia. Include facts and details from the article.

A Tiger's Life

_____

_____

_____

_____

_____

_____

_____

_____

_____

_____

_____

_____

_____

_____

Sampler Answer Key

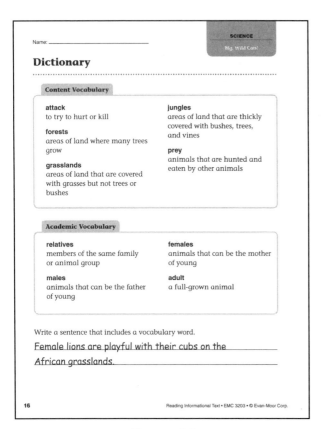

SCIENCE
Big, Wild Cats!

Dictionary

Content Vocabulary

attack
to try to hurt or kill

forests
areas of land where many trees grow

grasslands
areas of land that are covered with grasses but not trees or bushes

jungles
areas of land that are thickly covered with bushes, trees, and vines

prey
animals that are hunted and eaten by other animals

Academic Vocabulary

relatives
members of the same family or animal group

males
animals that can be the father of young

females
animals that can be the mother of young

adult
a full-grown animal

Write a sentence that includes a vocabulary word.
Female lions are playful with their cubs on the African grasslands.

16   Reading Informational Text • EMC 3203 • © Evan-Moor Corp.

Page 16

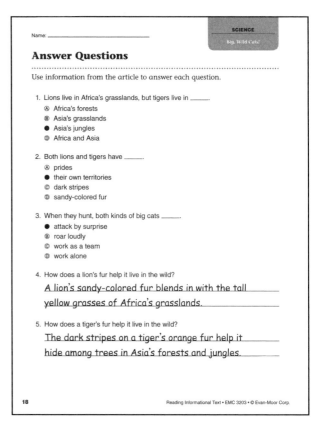

SCIENCE
Big, Wild Cats!

Answer Questions

Use information from the article to answer each question.

1. Lions live in Africa's grasslands, but tigers live in _____.
   - Ⓐ Africa's forests
   - Ⓑ Asia's grasslands
   - ● Asia's jungles
   - Ⓓ Africa and Asia

2. Both lions and tigers have _____.
   - Ⓐ prides
   - ● their own territories
   - Ⓒ dark stripes
   - Ⓓ sandy-colored fur

3. When they hunt, both kinds of big cats _____.
   - ● attack by surprise
   - Ⓑ roar loudly
   - Ⓒ work as a team
   - Ⓓ work alone

4. How does a lion's fur help it live in the wild?
   A lion's sandy-colored fur blends in with the tall yellow grasses of Africa's grasslands.

5. How does a tiger's fur help it live in the wild?
   The dark stripes on a tiger's orange fur help it hide among trees in Asia's forests and jungles.

18   Reading Informational Text • EMC 3203 • © Evan-Moor Corp.

Page 18

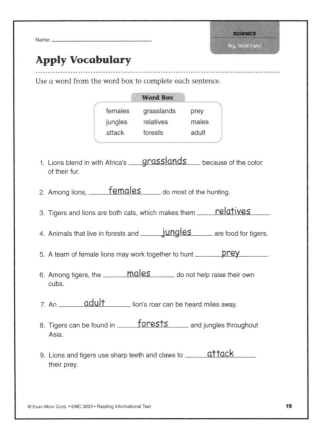

SCIENCE
Big, Wild Cats!

Apply Vocabulary

Use a word from the word box to complete each sentence.

Word Box

females	grasslands	prey
jungles	relatives	males
attack	forests	adult

1. Lions blend in with Africa's _grasslands_ because of the color of their fur.

2. Among lions, _females_ do most of the hunting.

3. Tigers and lions are both cats, which makes them _relatives_.

4. Animals that live in forests and _jungles_ are food for tigers.

5. A team of female lions may work together to hunt _prey_.

6. Among tigers, the _males_ do not help raise their own cubs.

7. An _adult_ lion's roar can be heard miles away.

8. Tigers can be found in _forests_ and jungles throughout Asia.

9. Lions and tigers use sharp teeth and claws to _attack_ their prey.

© Evan-Moor Corp. • EMC 3203 • Reading Informational Text   19

Page 19

SCIENCE
Big, Wild Cats!

Compare and Contrast

A text that has a **compare-and-contrast** structure is about two main ideas. It tells how the two ideas are alike (compares). It also tells how the two ideas are different (contrasts).

Authors use these signal words to create a **compare-and-contrast** structure:

Signal Words

both	today	but
long ago	however	unlike

1. The first paragraph tells us that the article will compare and contrast what two things?
   lions and tigers

2. Write the sentence that tells how tigers are different from lions in the way they live.
   Unlike lions, tigers do not live in groups.

3. Are lions and tigers alike or different in what they eat? Write the sentence from the article that tells you how they are similar or different.
   They are alike. Lions and tigers are meat eaters.

20   Reading Informational Text • EMC 3203 • © Evan-Moor Corp.

Page 20

Daily Language Review, Common Core Edition

Each book provides four or five items for every day of a 36-week school year. Skill areas include grammar, punctuation, mechanics, usage, and sentence editing. There are also scope and sequence charts, suggestions for use, and answer keys for the teacher. 136 pages.
Correlated to state and Common Core State Standards.

Teacher's Edition		Student Pack (5 Student Books)		Class Pack (20 Student Books + Teacher's Edition)	
Grade 1	EMC 579	Grade 1	EMC 6515	Grade 1	EMC 6521
Grade 2	EMC 580	Grade 2	EMC 6516	Grade 2	EMC 6522
Grade 3	EMC 581	Grade 3	EMC 6517	Grade 3	EMC 6523
Grade 4	EMC 582	Grade 4	EMC 6518	Grade 4	EMC 6524
Grade 5	EMC 583	Grade 5	EMC 6519	Grade 5	EMC 6525
Grade 6	EMC 576	Grade 6	EMC 6520	Grade 6	EMC 6526
Grade 7	EMC 2797	Grade 7	EMC 6597	Grade 7	EMC 9677
Grade 8	EMC 2798	Grade 8	EMC 6598	Grade 8	EMC 9678

Daily Math Practice, Common Core Edition

Grade appropriate, educationally sound, and designed to support your math curriculum. Based on NCTM standards, *Daily Math Practice, Common Core Edition* addresses key learning objectives including computation, problem solving, reasoning, geometry, measurement, and much more. Answer key and scope and sequence chart included. 128 pages.
Correlated to state and Common Core State Standards.

Teacher's Edition		Student Pack (5 Student Books)		Class Pack (20 Student Books + Teacher's Edition)	
Grade 1	EMC 750	Grade 1	EMC 6527	Grade 1	EMC 6533
Grade 2	EMC 751	Grade 2	EMC 6528	Grade 2	EMC 6534
Grade 3	EMC 752	Grade 3	EMC 6529	Grade 3	EMC 6535
Grade 4	EMC 753	Grade 4	EMC 6530	Grade 4	EMC 6536
Grade 5	EMC 754	Grade 5	EMC 6531	Grade 5	EMC 6537
Grade 6	EMC 755	Grade 6	EMC 6532	Grade 6	EMC 6538

Successful Students Practice at Home!

AWARD-WINNING*

SKILL SHARPENERS PreK–6

Connecting School & Home

Skill Sharpeners provides at-home practice that helps students master and retain skills. Each book in this dynamic series is the ideal resource for programs such as summer school, after school, remediation, school book fairs, and fundraising. 144 full-color pages.

- **activities aligned with national and state standards**
- **assessment pages in standardized-test format**
- **full-color, charmingly illustrated, and kid-friendly**

Spell & Write				Reading			
PreK	EMC 4535	3	EMC 4539	PreK	EMC 4527	3	EMC 4531
K	EMC 4536	4	EMC 4540	K	EMC 4528	4	EMC 4532
1	EMC 4537	5	EMC 4541	1	EMC 4529	5	EMC 4533
2	EMC 4538	6	EMC 4542	2	EMC 4530	6	EMC 4534

Math				Science			
PreK	EMC 4543	3	EMC 4547	PreK	EMC 5319	3	EMC 5323
K	EMC 4544	4	EMC 4548	K	EMC 5320	4	EMC 5324
1	EMC 4545	5	EMC 4549	1	EMC 5321	5	EMC 5325
2	EMC 4546	6	EMC 4550	2	EMC 5322	6	EMC 5326

"Colorful and fun! **Skill Sharpeners** *has successfully engaged my very easily distracted son. I highly recommend it."*

—Parent, Cambridge, Idaho

The National Parenting Center, Seal of Approval Winner

iParenting Media Awards Outstanding Product